MOTOR CYCLE
PASSION

teNeues

"Did you see the red light back there?"

—

"Well, you know, once you've seen a red light, you've seen 'em all."

From the movie
Drop dead Darling

„Hast du die rote Ampel eben gesehen?"

—

„Ach, eine rote Ampel sieht doch aus wie die andere."

Aus
Drop dead Darling

FOREWORD

ENJOY THE RIDE!

MICHAEL KÖCKRITZ

Passion! We meet it on the motorcycles, on a ride that's as much about obsession as amusement. No other modern technical inventions rival motorcycles; they turn our zest for freedom, longing for identity, and real experience into a way of life. Classic heritage and technical achievement: The motorcycle has always intensified our ability to live in the moment. Where else, apart from on a motorcycle, can you feel relaxed about traveling faster and looking cooler? This unique sense of freedom brings bikers together—and the majority of them seem like wild dogs, cool dudes, self-assured life embracers, and individuals with their own values, attitudes, hopes, and dreams. This is a community of free spirits, untroubled by the pace of modern life. They use motorcycles as a catalyst to drive their private ambitions.

And so to the heart of this book. It's a true celebration of the motorcycle in all its forms and a contrast to the automobile: Motorcycles are the essence of transport at its technical and minimal best, powered by functional design that can even seduce us with its aesthetic styling. Our awesome lineup of machines is destined to bring a glint to the reader's eye at the very sound of their names: Sleek lines of classic bikes, along with the upgraded, technical finesse of 21st century models; or custom bikes that reflect the harmony of creativity, design & technology, nostalgia, and progress. We remember the motorcycle heroes, who were not only champions of the racing circuit, but also crafted their legacy on the world's racetracks. We recall the most thrilling world championship motorcycle races; join in a captivating ride along the best scenic biker routes around the world. And as we explore the best shops with apparel for our motorcycling passion, we invite you to live the dream.

Leidenschaft! Hier ist sie. Und wir mittendrin. Natürlich auf dem Motorrad, was die Angelegenheit mitunter ebenso intensiv wie unterhaltsam macht. Denn wie bei keiner anderen technischen Erfindung der Neuzeit werden beim Motorrad Freiheit und die Sehnsucht nach Identität und authentischen Erfahrungen zum Lebensgefühl. Unsere Fähigkeit, in der Welt zu sein, hat das Motorrad ja schon immer technisch wunderbar verstärkt; nirgendwo sonst lässt sich das lässige, entspannte Unterwegssein besser und schneller ausleben als auf dem Bike. Eine Freiheit, die wiederum dazu führt, dass gerade unter den Motorradfahrern wilde Hunde, coole Typen und selbstbewusste Genießer in einem hohen Maße vertreten sind, Typen mit eigenen Werten, Haltungen und Lebensentwürfen. Menschen, die sich nicht so leicht irritieren lassen, von modernen Zeiten sowieso nicht, sondern die das Motorrad als Katalysator ihres eigenen inneren Antriebs verwenden.

VORWORT

Hiermit wären wir dann auch mittendrin in diesem Buch, in dem wir das Motorrad an sich feiern, dieses im Gegensatz zum Automobil auf das wesentliche, die pure technische Essenz reduzierte Fortbewegungsmittel, das mit einem wunderbar funktionellen Design zum ästhetischen Erlebnis werden kann. Den Beweis treten wir an, indem wir jene Maschinen zusammenführen, die uns schon allein aufgrund des Klangs ihres Namens ein Leuchten in die Augen zaubern: die Classic Bikes in all ihrer Geradlinigkeit ebenso wie die Motorräder des 21. Jahrhunderts mit ihren technischen Finessen; oder die Custom Bikes mit ihrer Kreativität, die Technik und Design, Nostalgie und Fortschritt so wunderbar in sich vereinen. Wir werfen einen Blick auf die Helden, die nicht nur im Kreis um die Wette gefahren sind, sondern sich auf den Rennstrecken der Welt ihr eigenes Denkmal errichtet haben. Wir blicken auf die besonderen Motorradtreffen dieser Welt, fahren auf den reizvollsten Biker-Routen durch Deutschland und einmal um die Welt. Und wir bummeln durch eine Reihe von Shops, die uns das richtige Outfit für unsere Leidenschaft versprechen. Leidenschaft, einmal ganzheitlich ausgelebt.

CONTENTS

014

BIKES AND HEROES

130

RIDES AND MEETS

178

CUSTOM BIKES AND SHOPS

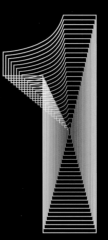

"We can't all be heroes because somebody has to sit on the curb and clap as they go by."

William Penn Adair
"Will" Rogers

„Wir können nicht alle Helden sein – weil ja irgendeiner am Bordstein stehen und klatschen muss, wenn sie vorüber-schreiten."

William Penn Adair
„Will" Rogers

FORGET ABOUT THE DO'S AND DON'TS. THIS IS ABOUT PASSION AND DESIRE, THE KIND OF PLEASURE THAT COMES ON TWO WHEELS. IT'S ABOUT MOTORCYCLES–CLASSIC AS WELL AS GENUINE FUTURE COLLECTOR ITEMS THAT USHERED IN NEW TRENDS AND INDEED NEW ERAS– AND THE ONGOING QUEST FOR MORE HORSEPOWER, SAFETY, AND CREATURE COMFORTS. MOREOVER, THIS CHAPTER REVEALS THE STORIES OF MOTORCYCLE RACERS–STORIES ABOUT RIVALRY UNLIKE ANY OTHER. HERE HEROES AREN'T MEASURED BY HOW MANY BONES THEY'VE BROKEN OR EVEN BY HOW MANY VICTORIES THEY'VE SCORED. IT'S ABOUT GETTING UP AFTER TAKING A FALL. GET READY FOR THE BIKES AND HEROES.

HIER GEHT ES NICHT UM RICHTIG ODER FALSCH. HIER GEHT ES UM LEIDENSCHAFT UND BEGIERDE, LUST AUF ZWEI RÄDERN. UM CLASSIC BIKES UND YOUNGTIMER, DIE ZU SAMMLERSTÜCKEN GEWORDEN SIND, WEIL SIE TRENDS GESETZT UND NEUE EPOCHEN EINGELEITET HABEN. UND UM DAS VERLANGEN NACH MEHR: PS, SICHERHEIT, KOMFORT. ERGÄNZT WIRD DAS KAPITEL DURCH GESCHICHTEN VON RENNFAHRERN. ALS KRÄFTEMESSEN DER BESONDEREN ART, DENN EIN HELD LÄSST SICH NICHT AN DER ZAHL SEINER KNOCHENBRÜCHE ODER SIEGE MESSEN. SONDERN AN SEINER TAPFERKEIT AUFZUSTEHEN, WENN ER MAL ABFLIEGT. EINE GANZ BESONDERE MOTORRAD- UND HELDENREISE.

The Bikes–Our Heroes

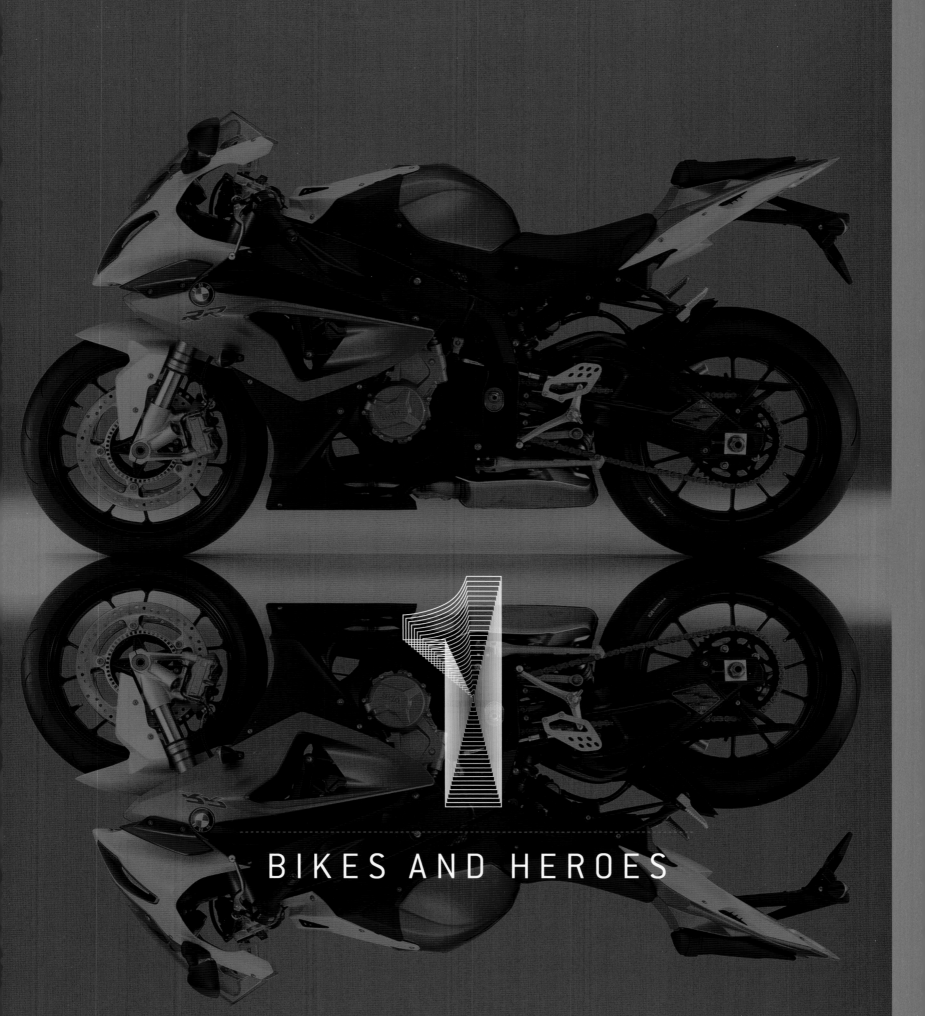

1

BIKES AND HEROES

APRILIA
RSV4 RR

TECH SPECS

ENGINE:

V4

POWER:

148 kW (201 hp) at 13,000 rpm

DISPLACEMENT:

999 cc

Timing is crucial when it comes to extreme sports bikes. So we must pay Aprilia a handsome compliment for first taking the World Superbike title, and then, only days later, for the launch of the new RSV4 RR at EICMA in Milan. A high-end racer with 201 hp—that's a high-level step up from its forerunner with its massively upgraded 65-degree V4 engine. The fact that the entire work of art also weighs in at 3¼ pounds lighter emphasizes how seriously the Italians take it, and as for its sound, the RSV is entirely in a league of its own, as always.

Timing ist eine wesentliche Komponente im Umgang mit sehr sportlichen Motorrädern. In diesem Punkt darf man Aprilia ein Kompliment machen: Erst der Superbike-WM-Titel und ein paar Tage später die Präsentation der neuen RSV4 RR auf der EICMA in Mailand. Ein High-End-Racer mit 201 PS, der mit seinem massiv überarbeitetem 65-Grad-V4 im Vergleich zum Vorgänger deutlich zulegt. Dass das Gesamtkunstwerk 1,5 kg abgespeckt hat, unterstreicht die Ernsthaftigkeit, mit der man es in Italien anpackt. Und soundtechnisch fuhr die RSV sowieso seit jeher in einer eigenen Liga.

APRILIA
RSV4 RF

TECH SPECS

ENGINE:

V4

POWER:

148 kW (201 hp) at 13,000 rpm

DISPLACEMENT:

999 cc

Let's get this straight: Telling the RR and the RF apart depends on just one letter of the alphabet. But that teeny alteration—from "R" to "F"—makes a world of difference. While the RR is a race-capable street version of the superbike, the RF is a street-capable race version. Or put it plainly: It's all a question of perspective. The RF, in a limited edition of 500 units, sends a crystal clear message in its Superpole paint scheme. Fitted with the Aprilia Race Pack as standard, it lines up on the grid with lighter forged rims and Öhlins chassis. It shares its engine and race-capable ABS with the RR.

Jetzt mag man einwerfen, es ist doch nur ein Buchstabe Unterschied zwischen der RR und der RF. Im Falle der Aprilia RSV4 ist der Unterschied zwischen dem „R" und dem „F" aber enorm. Denn während die RR die rennstreckentaugliche Straßenversion ist, handelt es sich bei der RF um die straßentaugliche Rennstreckenversion des Superbikes. Sprich: alles eine Frage der Perspektive. Die auf 500 Stück limitierte RF setzt im Superpole-Dekor deutliche Zeichen: serienmäßig mit dem Aprilia Race Pack ausgestattet, wartet sie unter anderem mit leichteren Schmiedefelgen und einem Öhlins-Fahrwerk an der Startampel. Motor und Race-ABS teilt sie sich mit der RR.

TECH SPECS

ENGINE:

V4

POWER:

129 kW (175 hp) at 11,000 rpm

DISPLACEMENT:

1,077 cc

Naked bikes is a truly deserved name, especially given their full reveal of the bare bones of a motorcycle. Take the Tuono V4 1100 RR, for example, it's more than justified to quote the naked statistics: With a displacement of 1,077 cc, the Tuono now produces 175 hp—that's 5 hp more than its predecessor. It generates 120 Newton meters of torque. Aprilia have also come up with improved traction control, wheelie control, launch control, and quick shift systems, as well as its race-capable ABS—all with multi-stage adjustments.

Naked Bikes haben sich ihren Namen nicht zuletzt deshalb verdient, weil sie den Blick freigeben auf die wesentlichen Dinge eines Motorrads. Umso mehr ist es gerechtfertigt, im Falle der Tuono V4 1100 RR schlicht die nackten Zahlen zu nennen: Aus 1077 cm³ Hubraum generiert die Tuono jetzt 175 PS, also fünf Pferde mehr als die Vorgängerin. Das Drehmoment liegt bei 120 Newtonmeter. Verbessert wurden zudem Traktionskontrolle, Wheelie-Kontrolle, Launch-Kontrolle und Schaltautomat sowie das renntaugliche ABS – alles ist in mehreren Stufen einstellbar.

APRILIA
Tuono V4 1100 RR

TECH SPECS

ENGINE:

V2

POWER:

92 kW (128 hp) at 8,000 rpm

DISPLACEMENT:

1,197 cc

The Caponord is a real balancing artist, something few rivals have ever achieved, and masterfully retains historic and future-oriented features. It pulled right away from the competition back in the late 1990s, and since its comeback in 2013, it has embraced state-of-the-art technology to link seamlessly with its classic history. Its 1,200-cc V2 engine and 128 hp makes the enduro designed for any road. Added to that are its adjustable handling settings from "Rain" or "Touring" to "Sport." This version is up for almost any road conditions, or almost any challenge.

Die Caponord schafft etwas, was sonst nur ganz wenigen gelingt: den Spagat zwischen Tradition und Zukunft. Schon Ende der Neunzigerjahre fuhr sie ihrer Konkurrenz davon, und seit ihrem Comeback 2013 knüpft sie mit modernster Technik nahtlos an diese Tradition an. Die Enduro ist mit einem 1200-cm³-V2 und 128 PS für jede Straßenlage geschaffen und dank wählbarer Fahrmodifikationen von „Regen" über „Touring" bis hin zu „Sport" auch für nahezu jede Straßenbeschaffenheit – beziehungsweise für nahezu jeden Anspruch.

APRILIA
Caponord 1200 Travel Pack

VALENTINO ROSSI

You know you've come a long way when you're considered a Living Legend of MotoGP at the age of 36. Naturally, Valentino Rossi has earned his fair share of nicknames, which include "Rossifumi," "Vale," and "Valentinik." However, most people probably know him by the moniker "The Doctor," because he's known for picking his competitors apart one by one. With 9 World Championship titles under his belt, this Italian pro has joined the list of the most successful motorcycle racing professionals in history. An extroverted and immensely popular media star, Valentino Rossi, following in the footsteps of his father Graziano Rossi, always starts out at number 46 in the 125, 250, and 500 cc World Championships. Had his mother had her way, Valentino would still be playing soccer today, while his father introduced him to go-cart racing. Switching to mini bikes, Valentino won his first race in 1991. Just four years later, he was hailed as Italy's Motorcycle Road Racing Champion on Aprilia. From there, he went on to take World Championship titles, dominate the 500 cc World Championship on Honda, win in MotoGP on Honda and Yamaha, suffer an open tibia fracture, make a strong comeback on Ducati, and return to Yamaha. And that's only the short version.

Auch nicht schlecht, mit 36 Jahren schon als lebende Legende der MotoGP zu gelten. Valentino Rossi hat noch so einige Kosenamen: „Rossifumi", „Vale", „Valentinik". Der wohl bekannteste ist „The Doctor", weil er seine Gegner regelrecht auf der Strecke zerlegt. Mit 9 Weltmeistertiteln zählt der Italiener zu den erfolgreichsten Motorradrennfahrern der Geschichte. Der extrovertierte und überaus beliebte Medienstar startet, wie schon sein Vater Graziano Rossi, schon immer mit der Nummer 46 in den Klassen 125 cm³, 250 cm³ und 500 cm³. Wenn es nach seiner Mutter gegangen wäre, würde Rossi heute kicken, sein Vater wiederum brachte ihn zum Kartfahren, bevor Valentino auf ein Minibike umstieg und damit im Jahr 1991 sein erstes Rennen gewann. Vier Jahre später feierte man ihn bereits als italienischen Motorrad-Straßenmeister auf Aprilia. Es folgten WM-Titel, Erfolge in der 500-cm³-Königsklasse auf Honda, Siege in der MotoGP-Klasse mit Honda und Yamaha, ein offener Schienbeinbruch, ein starkes Comeback auf Ducati und die Rückkehr zu Yamaha. Und das war nur die abgespeckte Version.

Some liked to call him "The Spaceman." Others had a more flattering nickname for him—"Fast Freddie." And Frederick Burdette Spencer was *fast*. In fact, he was fast in becoming fast: Signing up with Honda in 1983, he rode their factory bikes to become the youngest World Champion of all time at age 21. Two years later, he clinched two World Champion titles at once, leaving behind all his opponents during the 250 cc and 500 cc Championships. Unfortunately, his good luck streak ended there. What followed were various injuries and an attempted comeback in the year 1993, which would quickly prove to be a failure. It wasn't all bad, though: Since 1997, he has kept plenty busy running "Freddie Spencer's High Performance Riding School" in Las Vegas. Moreover, he can always take a trip down memory lane if he wants to, revisiting his 27 Grand Prix victories, 3 World Championship titles, as well as his place in the MotoGP Hall of Fame.

„Der Außerirdische", nannten sie ihn in der Szene. Oder, etwas charmanter, „Fast Freddie", denn schnell war er, Frederick Burdette Spencer. Und er war schon ziemlich früh ziemlich schnell: Im Jahr 1983 wurde er auf Honda bereits jüngster Weltmeister aller Zeiten. Mit 21 Jahren, wohlgemerkt. Zwei Jahre später feierte er zwei Weltmeistertitel auf einmal, als er in den Klassen 250 cm^3 und 500 cm^3 alle Gegner hinter sich ließ. Das war's dann aber leider mit der Glückssträhne. Was folgte, waren Verletzungen und der Versuch eines Comebacks im Jahr 1993, mit dem er schon schnell kläglich scheitern wird. Macht doch nichts, seit 1997 hat er ohnehin genug zu tun mit seiner „Freddie Spencer's High Performance Riding School" in Las Vegas. Und wenn er mag, kann er in der Vergangenheit schwelgen und auf 27 Grand-Prix-Siege, 3 Weltmeistertitel und seinen Platz in der MotoGP Hall of Fame zurückblicken.

 # FREDDIE SPENCER

The first bikes made in Japan in the 1950s and 1960s proved blatant copies of European models. In 1974, Italian manufacturer Benelli returned the favor by copying from Honda. The result was the Benelli 750 Sei. Or put it another way: The world's first six-cylinder street motorbike. It was a direct challenge to anything coming out of Japan, boasting 71 hp along with six exhaust pipes and a sound that was the antithesis of understatement. It was like giving each of the Sei's cylinders its own bullhorn! They wanted it loud, and loud it was. As loud as the provocation made by Benelli when the company founded by Alessandro de Tomaso heavily based its design of the Sei on the Honda CB 500 Four. Actually, that's putting it mildly, as the engine was more or less identical to that of the 500 Four.

Die ersten Nippon-Motorräder in den Fünfziger- und Sechzigerjahren waren freche Kopien europäischer Modelle. Dann aber spickte Benelli in Italien bei Honda. Was dabei herauskam, war 1974 die Benelli 750 Sei. Oder mit anderen Worten: die erste Sechszylinder-Straßenmaschine der Welt. Kampfansage Richtung Japan, mit 71 PS, sechs Auspuffrohren und einem Sound, der alles andere als Understatement war. Jeder Zylinder hatte quasi sein eigenes Megafon-Rohr. Laut sollte sie sein, so wie die Benellis Provokation, schließlich orientierte sich das Unternehmen von Alessandro de Tomaso beim Bau der Sei stark an der Honda CB 500 Four. Orientieren ist noch untertrieben, der 750er-Motor war nahezu identisch mit der 500er-Four made in Japan.

TECH SPECS

ENGINE:

Six-cylinder in-line, four-stroke

POWER:

52 kW (71 hp) at 8,900 rpm

DISPLACEMENT:

748 cc

PRODUCTION:

1974–1977

BENELLI
750 Sei

BIMOTA
SB 4

Trained ears will recognize the sound of a Suzuki GSX 1100 E from afar. But look real close and you'll discover the true character of some of these. Behold the Bimota SB 4 from 1984, which borrows the 112-hp 1,100-cc power plant of said Suzuki, while taking its frame to entirely new extremes. With the SB 4, Bimota created its masterpiece. Test reports from the time praised it as a work of art, referring not only to its remarkable looks, but also to its radical handling of the suspension with its 16-inch tires. Total production of the SB 4 numbered 272 units, 166 of which came with partial cowling as compared to the full cowling featured on the remaining units, known as SB 4S.

Geschulte Ohren erkennen den Sound einer Suzuki GSX 1100 E aus weiter Ferne. Doch bisweilen erschließt sich der wahre Motorradcharakter erst dann, wenn man den Sehsinn mit ins Boot holt. So baut die Bimota SB 4 von 1984 auf dem 112 PS starken 1100er-Motor besagter Suzuki auf, nimmt sich aber die Freiheit, mit dem Fahrgestell und dem Outfit eigene Wege zu gehen. Mit der SB 4 schuf Bimota damals sein Meisterstück. Zeitgenössische Testberichte schrieben von wahrer Kunst und meinten damit nicht nur die einzigartige Optik, sondern auch die Handlichkeit des neuen Fahrwerks mit 16-Zoll-Rädern. Von der SB4 wurden insgesamt nur 272 Edelbikes gebaut, 166 davon mit Teilverkleidung, der Rest als SB 4S mit Vollverkleidung.

TECH SPECS

ENGINE:

Four-cylinder in-line

POWER:

83 kW (112 hp) at 8,750 rpm

DISPLACEMENT:

1,075 cc

PRODUCTION:

1983–1984

The West German "Economic Miracle" brought unprecedented prosperity to virtually every German at the time, except for German motorcycle manufacturers. All of them went bankrupt, save for a few big ones—like BMW—that somehow managed to hang on. What happened? Well, more and more prosperous owners began proudly cruising around in their first brand new automobiles. They may have been tiny and rather cramped inside, but at least their riders were no longer exposed to the elements. As a basic ride, motorcycles were effectively out of the picture at this point. In perfect sync, across the great pond, motorcycles were seen in a wholly different light and underwent a remarkable revival as symbols of freedom. Back in Europe, BMW was quick to rise to the occasion, turning its humble R 60 Boxer into the 42-hp R 69 S and making it one of the world's fastest and most beautiful motorcycles of the 1960s. It was also famous-notorious for initial engine busts, which remained a problem until the introduction of vibration dampers in 1963.

Die deutschen Motorradhersteller fluchten in den Sechzigerjahren über die Früchte des Wirtschaftswunders. Nur ein paar Große überlebten mit Ach und Krach, darunter BMW. Was war passiert? Die Bundesbürger fuhren stolz ihren ersten eigenen Wagen spazieren – klein zwar, eng vielleicht, aber mit Dach überm Kopf. Das Motorrad als Gefährt hatte bei uns ausgedient. Anders in den USA: Dort feierte das Bike fröhliche Urständ als Freiheitssymbol. Die Bayern reagierten und schneiderten aus dem gemächlichen R 60-Boxer die 42 PS starke R 69 S. In den Sechzigerjahren eine der schnellsten und auch schönsten Maschinen. Die anfänglichen Motorplatzer waren fast schon legendär, ehe ein Schwingungsdämpfer an der Kurbelwelle ab 1963 Abhilfe schuf.

BMW MOTORRAD
R 69 S

TECH SPECS

ENGINE:

Boxer twin, four-stroke

POWER:

31 kW (42 hp) at 7,000 rpm

DISPLACEMENT:

595 cc

PRODUCTION:

1960–1969

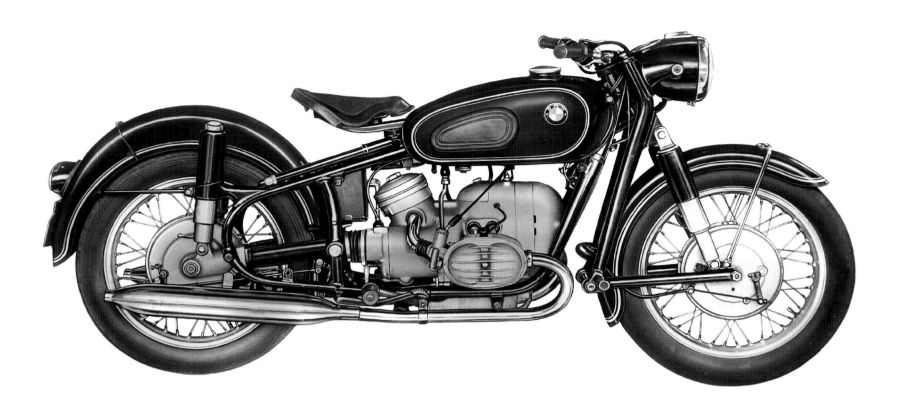

TECH SPECS

ENGINE:

Boxer twin, four-stroke

POWER:

19 kW (26 hp) at 5,800 rpm

DISPLACEMENT:

494 CC

PRODUCTION:

1955–1969

BMW MOTORRAD
R 50

BMW wrote its own chapter in the West German economic recovery phenomenon when it came out with a new motorcycle, the R 50, in 1955. Powered by a two-cylinder Boxer engine capable of 26 hp, it embodied the spirit of a new generation. It had been a long time since BMW introduced the concept of straight-line rear suspension back in 1938, which also marked the last time of any real development on motorcycle suspensions. With the launch of its R 50 model at the Brussels Motor Show, BMW changed its paradigm by presenting a model with an innovative twin-loop frame. This made the R 50 such a stable ride that it seemed glued to the pavement. Due to this, the new Boxer's nickname in the US was "King of the Road."

BMW schrieb 1955 sein eigenes Kapitel vom Wirtschaftswunder, als im Januar die R 50 vom Band rollte. Das Motorrad mit dem Zweizylinder-Boxermotor war mit 26 PS ausgestattet und verkörperte den Geist einer neuen BMW-Generation. Seit 1938, also jenem Jahr, in dem das Werk die Geradeweg-Hinterradfederung einführte, hatte man sich kaum noch um eine Verbesserung des Fahrwerks bemüht. Mit der erstmals auf dem Salon in Brüssel vorgestellten R 50 änderte BMW sein Paradigma und präsentierte ein Modell, das ein neuartiges Vollschwingenfahrwerk besaß. Derart ausgestattet, schien die R 50 auf der Straße zu kleben. Die hervorragende Fahrstabilität verhalf dem neuen Boxer in den USA zum Titel „King of the Road".

In the mid-1970s, BMW went into the offensive with a whole range of new models. One of them stood out from the rest: The R 100 RS. It featured full body cladding that had been wind tunnel tested, was firmly fixed to the frame, and weighed just 21 pounds—an industry first at its appearance back in 1976. Debuting as such in Bavaria that year, the R 100 RS presented itself as a revolution on two wheels, a 70-hp sport bike that took its riders into a whole new realm of possibilities. Not only did its body cladding protect against wind and rain, it further improved aerodynamic and thus handling characteristics, helping riders maintain control even when reaching 125 mph top speed.

Mitte der Siebzigerjahre ging BMW mit einer ganzen Palette an neuen Modellen in die Offensive. Eines stach aus der Menge heraus: die R 100 RS. Eine im Windkanal entwickelte Vollverkleidung – fest mit dem Rahmen verbunden und nur 9,5 Kilo schwer – das hatte die Branche anno 1976 noch nicht gesehen. So präsentierte sich die R 100 RS bei ihrer Vorstellung in Bayern als eine Revolution auf zwei Rädern. Als eine 70 PS starke Sportmaschine, die den Fahrer in neue Bereiche des Möglichen mitnahm. Nicht nur vor Wind und Wetter bot die Verkleidung Schutz, sie verbesserte auch die Aerodynamik und damit die Fahrdynamik. Locker wurde ein Topspeed von 200 km/h erreicht.

TECH SPECS

ENGINE:

Boxer twin, four-stroke

POWER:

52 kW (70 hp) at 7,250 rpm

DISPLACEMENT:

980 cc

PRODUCTION:

1976–1984

BMW MOTORRAD
R 100 RS

TECH SPECS

ENGINE:

Boxer twin, four-stroke

POWER:

50 kW (67 hp) at 7,000 rpm

DISPLACEMENT:

898 cc

PRODUCTION:

1973–1976

BMW MOTORRAD
R 90 S

Don't mess with Bavaria—the company from Germany's Free State came up with the BMW R 90 S in response to fierce competition primarily out of Japan and Italy. This was when Honda had a winner with the CB 750 Four, Kawasaki had one with the Z 900 Z1, Suzuki with the 750 GT while the Italian manufacturers were riding high on the Moto Guzzi GT 85 0L, Ducati 750 SS and Laverda 750 SS. The shaft drive of the R 90 S made it the first machine to hit almost 125 mph with five gears. It used front disc brakes, which safely kept the BMW from penetrating too deep into its newly discovered speed dimension. Another world premiere featuring on BMW's new superbike at the time was its glass-fiber reinforced cockpit cowl, fitted to the handlebar, and the tail on its back.

Man sollte sie halt nicht reizen, die Bayern: Mit der BMW R 90 S reagierten die Freistaatler 1973 auf die starke Konkurrenz, vor allem aus Japan und Italien: Honda kam damals mit der CB 750 Four, Kawasaki mit der Z 900 Z1, Suzuki mit der 750 GT und die Herrschaften vom Stiefel ritten auf der Moto Guzzi GT 850 L, Ducati 750 SS oder Laverda 750 SF daher. Der Kardanantrieb schob den Sport-Boxer R 90 S erstmals über fünf Gänge auf fast 200 km/h. Eine Doppelscheibenbremsanlage am Vorderrad verzögerte zuverlässig diese neue Fahrdimension. Weitere Neuheiten des Münchner Sportlers: die lenkerfeste Cockpitverkleidung aus glasfaserverstärktem Kunststoff und der freche Bürzel am Heck.

The point wasn't to create just another high-tuned, street-legal bullet bike. No, the point was to create an "easy handling high-tech masterpiece." That comment was made by the BMW managers about launching their K 1 model at the 1988 international tradeshow for bicycles and motorcycles IFMA in Cologne, Germany. As with all K models, this one had an in-line four under the gas tank. Following the basic philosophy of "doing everything possible," the K 1's 4-valve fuel-injected was the first to feature a catalytic converter. Add to that ABS for secure braking. The wrap-around cowl was one of the first of its kind and, as such, a bold move by BMW designers. Boasting a rated top speed of 150 mph, it nevertheless failed to attract buyers and sales were disappointing. Judging by its visual design and technology, the K 1 ultimately proved to be too far ahead of its time.

Sie wollten keine hochgezüchtete Rennmaschine mit Straßen-zulassung, sondern ein „beherrschbares High-Tech-Meisterwerk" konstruieren – so das Selbstverständnis der BMW-Manager bei der Vorstellung ihrer neuen K 1 auf der IFMA 1988 in Köln. Wie bei allen K-Modellen arbeitete ein Vierzylinder-Reihenmotor unter dem Tank. Nach dem Motto „machen, was machbar ist" war der Vierventil-Einspritzmotor erstmalig mit G-Kat ausgestattet, für sicheres Bremsen sorgte ein ABS. Mutig war die Rundum-Vollverkleidung, eine der ersten ihrer Art. Dem liegenden Gasgeber ermöglichte sie zwar echte 240 km/h Spitze, geliebt und vor allem gekauft wurde sie trotzdem leider nicht. Optisch und technisch war die K 1 ihrer Zeit zu weit voraus.

BMW MOTORRAD
K 1

TECH SPECS

ENGINE:

Four-cylinder in-line, four-stroke

POWER:

74 kW (100 hp) at 8,000 rpm

DISPLACEMENT:

987 CC

PRODUCTION:

1988–1993

TECH SPECS

ENGINE:

Three-cylinder in-line, four-stroke

POWER:

55 kW (75 hp) at 8,500 rpm

DISPLACEMENT:

740 CC

PRODUCTION:

1985–1996

BMW MOTORRAD
K 75

In 1985, Hans-Peter Briegel was named German Soccer Player of the Year. Not that Hans-Peter ever excelled at anything; he could just be counted on to do a good job at everything else. In that sense, call it a sign of the times when BMW's K 75 suddenly burst upon the market scene the same year. At first glance, the K 75 was the bipedal equivalent of the dependable soccer player: Angular, somewhat hulking, fascination factor near zero. On second glance, forget the first glance. This bike was dependable, all right, but it also revealed a soft side and, indeed, a passionate side. The K 75 was easygoing when you cracked the throttle and powerful when you insisted, its ride simply harmonious. Its front design was par for the course in the 1980s. A touch of neon here, a touch of black there, throw in some chrome, and that sucker was good to go!

Der deutsche Fußballer des Jahres 1985 hieß Hans-Peter Briegel. Die „Walz aus der Pfalz" konnte zwar nichts am besten, aber vieles gut. So gesehen war es vielleicht der Odem des Zeitgeistes, der die 750er-Dreizylinder K 75 im selben Jahr mitten ins Marktgeschehen blies. Sie war sozusagen das maschinelle Abbild des zuverlässigen Hans-Peters: kantig, fast sperrig, Blutwallungsfaktor gegen null. Doch der zweite Blick widersprach dem ersten entschieden. Hier herrschte Zuverlässigkeit, Weichheit, Leidenschaft. Und so betörte die K 75 mit ihrer Sanftheit am Gas, ihrer Kraft im Vorwärtsstreben, ihrer Harmonie im Fahrverhalten. Das Antlitz war in den Achtzigerjahren kein Problem. Ein bisschen Neon hier, ein bisschen Schwarz da, etwas Chrom, und fertig war die Laube.

TECH SPECS

ENGINE:

Parallel twin

POWER:

63 kW (85 hp) at 7,500 rpm

DISPLACEMENT:

798 cc

No matter how far your journey takes you, and no matter what surface the F 800 GS rolls on, its label "Adventure" is not a straight marketing ploy, but also a badge of distinction. The parallel twin generates 85 hp and 83 Newton meters of torque that, thanks to the 6.3-gallon tank and 55 miles-per-gallon fuel consumption at 56 mph, makes the kind of distances feasible that were only ever really a talking point for long-distance truckers at highway service rest areas.

Egal wie weit die Reise auch sein mag, egal welcher Untergrund sich vor diesem Bike ausbreitet, die F 800 GS trägt den Zusatz „Adventure" nicht aus Marketinggründen, sondern als Auszeichnung. 85 PS generieren aus dem Parallel-Twin 83 Newtonmeter Drehmoment und dank 24 Litern Tankvolumen und einem Verbrauch von 4,3 Litern bei 90 km/h sind Distanzen möglich, über die sich sonst nur Fernfahrer an der Raststätte unterhalten.

BMW MOTORRAD
F 800 GS Adventure

⭐ EVEL KNIEVEL

Who hasn't heard of Evel Knievel before? Anybody out there who hasn't obviously never heard what Roger Moore had to say in the old James Bond classic *The Man With the Golden Gun*, never played a game of *Stunt Cycle*, or listened to New Model Army and their album *Between Dog and Wolf*. In fact, it's almost impossible not to come across the name Robert Craig "Evel" Knievel at some point in life, considering that this American hero has become a household name. Because he showed us he could get on a motorbike and jump over more than 50 cars, because he was the biggest daredevil on two wheels to ever travel the earth, because he wasn't afraid to take on either the fountains at Caesars Palace in Las Vegas or Snake River Canyon in Idaho. Because he could do it like nobody else could. Until Wembley Stadium, London, May 26, 1975, when his attempt to jump more than 13 busses failed before an audience of 90,000. Following the failed jump, Evel Knievel promptly announced his retirement, having suffered a fractured hip and never even flinching. Did he remain standing throughout the ordeal? *You bet.*

Schon mal was von Evel Knievel gehört? Wer diese Frage mit Nein beantwortet, hat Roger Moore im James-Bond-Film *Der Mann mit dem goldenen Colt* nicht zugehört, noch nie *Stunt Cycle* gezockt und nicht das Album *Between Dog and Wolf* von New Model Army durchgehört. An Robert Craig „Evel" Knievel vorbeizukommen, ist schwierig, schließlich war der Amerikaner bekannt wie ein bunter Hund. Weil er auf seinem Bike über fünfzig Autos springen konnte, weil sich niemand auf zwei Rädern mehr traute, weil er weder vor der Brunnenanlage des Caesars Palace in Las Vegas noch vor dem Snake River Canyon zurückschreckte. Weil er es konnte wie kein anderer. Bis er versuchte, über 13 Busse zu springen. Und vor 90.000 Zuschauern scheiterte. Nach dem misslungenen Sprung kündigte er sofort seinen Rücktritt an. Im Londoner Wembley-Stadion. Mit gebrochener Hüfte. Ohne einen Mucks. Im Stehen. Eh klar.

 # SUE FISH

Five cervical spine surgeries, various head injuries, numerous fractures. It's all in a day's work when you're living on the edge. Or riding on the edge, as it were. Which is how Sue "Flying" Fish likes it. Never one to slow down, she has pushed both her bike and herself to the limits (and beyond). As the winner of the 1976 and '77 Motocross Championship and a stunt actress, it's not uncommon for her to casually smile every time her friends become worried when they can't reach her on the phone and start jamming her voice-mail with all kinds of hysterical messages. Oh, you never heard of Sue Fish before? Well, even if you've never heard of her, chances are, you've seen this fast-riding lady before. Among others, she was the stunt double for actress Linda Hamilton in *The Terminator*. Although quasi retired since 2009, she remains active as a personal trainer. In 2012, Sue Fish was inducted into the AMA Motorcycle Hall of Fame. What else is there to say? Fly on, Sue "Flying" Fish.

Fünf Operationen an der Halswirbelsäule, verschiedene Kopfverletzungen, zahlreiche Knochenbrüche. Was man eben so hat, wenn man am Limit lebt. Oder besser gesagt, am Limit fährt. Sue „Flying" Fish lebt gerne ein solches Leben. Fährt schnell, übertreibt es auf ihrem Bike und belächelt ihre Freunde, wenn sie sie mal wieder nicht telefonisch erreichen und sich Sorgen machen. Und den Anrufbeantworter der ehemaligen Motocross-Fahrerin und Stunt-Schauspielerin hysterisch vollquatschen. Sie kennen Sue Fish nicht? Also zumindest indirekt haben Sie die schnelle Dame sicherlich schon einmal gesehen, zum Beispiel als Stunt-Double für Linda Hamilton in *The Terminator*. Seit 2009 arbeitet sie – quasi im Ruhestand – als Personal Trainerin. Im Jahr 2012 wurde Fish in die AMA Motorcycle Hall of Fame aufgenommen. Was soll man dazu noch sagen? Fly on, Sue „Flying" Fish. Chapeau!

TECH SPECS

ENGINE:

V4

POWER:

148 kW (199 hp) at 13,500 rpm

DISPLACEMENT:

999 cc

This is by far the world's best-selling superbike. A classic build, though with top-level technical equipment, the latest version now offers electronic aids that allow lean angles of more than 40 degrees, even on wet roads, or even handle downshifting for you in Pro-Mode, so that both hands stay firmly on the handlebars under extremely hard braking maneuvers. At its heart, however, it still beats the four-cylinder engine, producing 199 hp, and coping with almost any situation with total nonchalance.

Sie ist das mit Abstand am besten verkaufte Superbike der Welt. Konventionell aufgebaut, aber technisch hochgerüstet bietet sie in der neusten Überarbeitung nun unter anderem auch elektronische Helfer, die mehr als 40 Grad Schräglage bei feuchtem Untergrund ermöglichen, oder im Pro-Modus sogar das Runterschalten übernehmen, sodass bei extrem harten Anbremsmanövern beide Hände vollständig am Griff bleiben können. Herzstück aber bleibt der Vierzylinder, der nun mit 199 PS jeder Lage fast schon erhaben begegnet.

BMW MOTORRAD
S 1000 RR

15

TECH SPECS

BMW MOTORRAD
S 1000 XR

ENGINE:

Four-cylinder in-line

POWER:

118 kW (160 hp) at 9,250 rpm

DISPLACEMENT:

999 cc

Let's take two race experts—the S 1000 RR and the HP4—add a third, the S 1000 R roadster, and team up with the fourth S 1000 XR model using the well-known 999-cc in-line four. XR features include vastly improved touring capability and overall superior riding comfort, so it's clearly designed with a different audience in mind, and also a bid to steal market share from Ducati's Multistrada. The striking technical difference is obviously the suspension: The XR has slightly under to over an inch more travel than its sisters. The XR's four-cylinder engine generates 160 hp and 112 Newton meters of torque.

Neben den beiden Race-Experten S 1000 RR und HP4 sowie dem Roadster S 1000 R ist die S 1000 XR das vierte Modell mit dem bekannten 1000er-Reihenvierzylinder. Mit deutlich erhöhter Tourentauglichkeit und mehr Fahrkomfort zielt die XR allerdings auf ein anderes Publikum und direkt in Richtung Multistrada von Ducati. Technisch machen sich die Unterschiede vor allem bei den Federwegen bemerkbar, bei denen die XR um 20 bis 30 mm gegenüber ihren Schwestern zulegt. Der Vierzylinder leistet in der XR 160 PS und generiert 112 Newtonmeter Drehmoment.

A city bike? Or an open road bike? Well, what about a bike for newbies? BMW's endeavor to come up with a response for all these questions is its water-cooled parallel twin F 800 R. This lightweight naked bike has a twin, four-stroke in-line engine producing 86 Newton meters of torque at 87 hp, with LED technology and a host of luggage options. A slight forward-leaning riding position turns the F 800 R into a perfect companion for long-distance travel and makes for awesome sports cornering. Compared to that, there is the alternative beginner's version available as a reduced power 34-hp model.

Ein Bike für die Stadt? Ein Bike für die Landstraße? Ein Bike für Einsteiger? Mit der wassergekühlten Parallel Twin F 800 R strebt BMW die Antwort auf jede dieser Fragen an. Ein leichtes Naked Bike mit Zweizylinder-Viertakt-Reihenmotor, 86 Newtonmeter bei 87 PS, LED-Technik und diversen Gepäcklösungen. Dank leicht nach vorne gebeugter Sitzposition eignet sich die F 800 R sowohl für lange Touren, als auch für die etwas sportlichere Kurvenhatz. Alternativ gibt es das Bike für Zweiradeinsteiger auch mit reduzierten 34 PS.

TECH SPECS

ENGINE:

Parallel twin

POWER:

64 kW (87 hp) at 8,000 rpm

DISPLACEMENT:

798 cc

BMW MOTORRAD
F 800 R

TECH SPECS

BMW MOTORRAD
K 1600 GLT

ENGINE:

Six-cylinder in-line

POWER:

118 kW (160 hp) at 7,750 rpm

DISPLACEMENT:

1,649 cc

The GLT presents on two wheels what the BMW 7-series offers on four: Luxury for long tours. Design features are all honed so that the rider feels lulled into a sense of ease and comfort over a long-distance run. The relaxed riding position for both rider and passenger, together with duolever front suspension and paralever at the rear, are perfect for easygoing cruising. With the ESA II (Electronic Suspension Adjustment) it can even be optimized at the touch of a button, damping and rebound can both be adjusted to suit the route and the rider.

Was der 7er-BMW auf vier Rädern ist, ist die GLT auf zwei Rädern: Luxus für lange Reisen. Alles ist darauf ausgelegt, bequem und komfortabel Strecke zurückzulegen. Eine entspannte Sitzposition, sowohl für den Fahrer als auch für den Beifahrer, kombiniert mit einem Fahrwerk aus Duolever-Vorderradführung und einer Paralever am Heck, sind auf entspanntes Dahingleiten ausgelegt. Optional kann das über das ESA II (Electronic Suspension Adjustment) per Knopfdruck sogar noch optimiert werden, da sich hier Dämpfung und Federung je nach Situation und Vorliebe einstellen lassen.

Those were the days when the name "BMW" was associated with motorcycles as much as with automobiles today. The R 51 RS now enjoys cult status, but the R 90 can be called a legend, too. It's only natural that there are more deafening calls for a retro bike, especially after design company RSD gave these demands a motorcycle face with the one-off R 90 S. With its R nineT, BMW has slipped into a vintage costume a boxer twin with 1,170 cc and 110 hp of modern performance.

Es gab eine Zeit, da baute BMW so selbstverständlich Motorräder wie heute Autos. Eine R 51 RS genießt heute Kultstatus, aber auch die R 90 darf sich das Legendenetikett an den Tank heften. Da ist es nur nachvollziehbar, dass die Rufe nach einem Retro-Bike immer lauter wurden, vor allem, nachdem die Firma RSD mit dem Einzelstück R 90 S dem Verlangen ein Motorradgesicht gegeben hat. Mit der R nineT schiebt BMW einen Zweizylinder-Boxer hinterher, der mit 1170 cm³ Hubraum und 110 PS moderne Fahrleistungen in ein Vintage-Kostüm packt.

TECH SPECS

ENGINE:

Boxer twin

POWER:

81 kW (110 hp) at 7,600 rpm

DISPLACEMENT:

1,170 cc

BMW MOTORRAD
R nineT

TECH SPECS

ENGINE:

Boxer twin

POWER:

92 kW (125 hp) at 7,750 rpm

DISPLACEMENT:

1,170 cc

Enter the new R 1200 R: BMW is now moving away from its classic styling towards a more edgy look. The headlamp, a short tail, and beefy muffler equal the new version of this naked roadster. After all, the retro department has clearly been expertly guided by the R nineT. When it comes to the engine, it uses the 125-hp water-cooled boxer that debuted in the big GS enduro in 2013. To maintain the naked R 1200 R's sleek lines, BMW has done away with the double radiators and opted for a central radiator that makes it necessary, once again, to move the monoshock.

Mit der neuen R 1200 R geht BMW weg vom klassischen Look, hin zu mehr Ecken und Kanten. Schweinwerfer, ein knappes Heck und bullige Endschalldämpfer definieren den Ausdruck des unverkleideten Roadsters. Die Retro-Abteilung wird schließlich bestens von der R nineT angeführt. Antriebstechnisch gibt es den wassergekühlten Boxer mit 125 PS, der 2013 in der Groß-Enduro GS debütierte. Um die schlanke Linie der nackten R 1200 R beizubehalten, verzichtete BMW aber auf die Doppelkühler und setzt auf einen zentralen Wasserkühler, der wiederum das Zentralfederbein verdrängt.

BMW MOTORRAD
R 1200 R

Whether for tackling whole countries or even continents, for ambitious riders planning to take their bikes on tour for more than just an afternoon's drive, say maybe for an entire month, ever since 2002 BMW has offered the Adventure model alongside its proven GS. The famed actor Ewan McGregor and his buddy, the actor Charley Boorman, even completed the ultimate round-the-world expedition on their bikes back in 2004. In comparison with the GS, the Adventure has a larger tank, longer suspension travel, and weighs more. It also comes fitted with a number of additional protectors.

Ob ganze Länder oder gar Kontinente – allen, die nicht nur für einen Nachmittag, sondern gleich für einen ganzen Monat auf das Bike steigen wollen, bietet BMW seit 2002 neben der bewährten GS auch die Adventure-Version an. Der Schauspieler Ewan McGregor umrundete gemeinsam mit seinem Freund Charley Boorman 2004 damit sogar die ganze Welt. Im Vergleich zur GS zeichnen die Adventure vor allem ein größerer Tank, längere Federwege und mehr Gewicht aus. Zudem verfügt sie über ein paar zusätzliche Protektoren.

TECH SPECS

ENGINE:

Boxer twin

POWER:

92 kW (125 hp) at 7,750 rpm

DISPLACEMENT:

1,170 cc

BMW MOTORRAD
R 1200 GS Adventure

TECH SPECS

ENGINE:

Two-cylinder in-line,

four-stroke

POWER:

36 kW (48 hp) at 6,250 rpm

DISPLACEMENT:

654 CC

PRODUCTION:

1965–1972

BSA
A65L 650 Lightning

Back in 1965, the 650 Lightning was Birmingham-based motorcycle manufacturer's attempt to produce a dependable bike for the US market, guaranteed trouble-free and free of oil puddles forming under its new engine. Well, that's an understatement! Prior to becoming a cult bike, her in-line twin made this gal one tough ride. Boasting 48 hp and easily capable of 105 mph, this bike had a way of making your fillings rattle. That's because all the action going on under the gas tank roughly felt like that of a jackhammer. And that was mild compared to its two siblings, the Lightning Clubman, which delivered 51 hp, and the Spitfire, which produced a whopping 55 hp—with engine vibrations rising accordingly. Some experts couldn't resist referring to them as real bikes for real men and praising their twin power plants to high heaven. Either way, the end of BSA was a foregone conclusion by 1973.

Mit der 650er Lightning wollte die Birminghamer Motorradschmiede 1965 eigentlich ein zuverlässiges Bike für den USA-Markt bauen. Ohne technische Panne, ohne Ölpfütze unter dem neuen Blockmotor. Von wegen! Bevor die Lady zum Kult wurde, machte es der Twin dem Cowboy schwer. 48 PS stark und gut 170 Sachen schnell, blieben nur mit viel Glück die Zahnplomben drin. Denn was sich unter dem Tank abspielte, ließ sich mit den Schlägen eines Presslufthammers vergleichen. Doch es sollte noch dicker kommen. Die Lightning Clubman brachte 51 PS, die Spitfire sogar 55 PS – und dazu noch mehr Vibrationen. Experten sprachen von echten Männer-Bikes und lobten die Powertwins hoch in den Himmel. Das Ende von BSA anno 1973 war jedoch längst vorprogrammiert.

In the early 1960s, the western world seemed to unwind. Dancing to the tunes of rock 'n' roll, people began to shake off the dust of the old ways, leather gave way to tweed, and ducktails were replacing crew cuts. Volkswagen Beetles and Mini Coopers were within everyone's budget, while the image of motorcycles went from basic transportation to the symbol of freedom to ride, especially in America. Soon an entire generation of free spirits began crisscrossing the nation's highways on two wheels. Catering to these individuals in particular, the British motorcycle maker BSA produced the A10 R Super Rocket: It was powerful, fast, and sexy. A true sports bike, especially in the face of more conservative legends like the Harley-Davidson and Indian.

Die westliche Welt geriet Anfang der Sechzigerjahre aus den Fugen: Der Rock 'n' Roll klopfte den Staub aus den Kleidern, Leder ersetzte Tweed, die Tolle den Bürstenhaarschnitt. Der Käfer und der Mini wurden für jedermann erschwinglich. Das Zweirad wandelte sein Image vom Transportmittel zum Freiheitssymbol für die „halbstarken" Motorradfans, vor allem in den USA. Eine junge Generation verrückter Individualisten bretterte auf dicken Feuerstühlen über die Highways. Für sie baute BSA aus Birmingham die A10 R Super Rocket: stark, schnell, sexy. Ein echtes Sportbike gegen die konservativen Legenden von Harley-Davidson und Indian.

TECH SPECS

ENGINE:

Two-cylinder in-line, two-stroke

POWER:

36 kW (48 hp) at 6,250 rpm

DISPLACEMENT:

646 CC

PRODUCTION:

1957–1963

BSA
A10 R 650 Super Rocket

To fully appreciate the magic of this machine, which was launched back in 1973, we need to look at the 200 Miles Race of Imola in 1972. Ducati made its racing debut here with a tuned-up street version of its 750 street model. Having shown little interest in entering the world of racing before, the company seemingly came out of nowhere and promptly began running circles around the usual heavyweights like Honda, Norton, Triumph, and even MV Agusta with multiple World Champion Giacomo Agostini. Double victory! Paul Smart followed by Bruno Spaggiari—it was a key moment for the Ducatisti: From then on, the company committed to building super racing machines, which it still does today.

Um den Zauber dieses ab 1973 verkauften Superbikes zu verstehen, muss man das 200-Meilen-Rennen von Imola 1972 beleuchten. Ducati trat dort als Außenseiter mit getunten 750er-Straßenmaschinen an. Aus dem Stand fuhr man den übermächtigen Werksrennern von Honda, Norton, Triumph und sogar MV Agusta mit Multi-Weltmeister Giacomo Agostini um die Ohren. Der Sieger hieß Paul Smart, Zweiter wurde Bruno Spaggiari. Ein Schlüsselmoment für die Ducatisti. Fortan kümmerte sich das italienische Werk um die populäre Superbike-Klasse. Bis heute.

TECH SPECS

ENGINE:

V2, four-stroke

POWER:

53 kW (72 hp) at 8,800 rpm

DISPLACEMENT:

748 cc

PRODUCTION:

1973–1974

DUCATI
750 SS

TECH SPECS

ENGINE:

V2, four-stroke

POWER:

59 kW (80 hp) at 7,000 rpm

DISPLACEMENT:

864 cc

PRODUCTION:

1975–1982

DUCATI
900 SS

Italians are known for their lifelong devotion to la dolce vita. How else do you explain their love for certain Italian brands back in the 1970s? Particularly when it comes to the Ducati 750 SS, not just because of its looks but also because of the technology behind it. No other bike out there could boast the same slim V2 frame, featuring line shafts in addition to overhead camshafts and desmodromic valves. The 750 SS was the first bona fide superbike for the streets. Its heir apparent in 1975 was the Ducati 900 SS, now boasting 80 hp, and it wasn't by accident that its looks carried over from the successful 750 SS. Rather, it was Ducati's way of paying homage to its sensational 1972 victory at the 200 Miles Race at Imola.

Der Italiener weiht der Schönheit sein Leben, anders ließ sich in den Siebzigerjahren die Liebe zu bestimmten einheimischen Motorradmarken nicht erklären. Eine besondere Stellung nahm die Ducati 750 SS ein. Optisch, aber vor allem technisch. Keine andere Maschine verfügte über einen so schlanken V2-Motor, mit Königswellen zu den obenliegenden Nockenwellen und desmodromischer Ventilsteuerung. Die 750 SS war das erste echte Superbike für den Straßenbetrieb. Die logische Nachfolgerin war 1975 die nun 80 PS starke Ducati 900 SS. Ganz bewusst hatte das Werk die Optik der erfolgreichen 750 SS übernommen. In ehrender Erinnerung an den sensationellen Sieg beim 200-Meilen-Rennen 1972 in Imola.

 # DOUG POLEN

Doug Polen's track record speaks for itself: 27 wins out of 80 races in the World Superbike, which translates into more than one out of three races. Born in 1960, this former motorcycle racing pro has earned a permanent spot on the heroes' list of many. His career was already well underway in the AMA Superbike Championship during the early 1980s before he withdrew from racing for a couple of years. Returning for the 1988 season, he entered the races on a Yoshimura-Suzuki factory bike, winning both the TT-F1 and TT-F3 Championships in the following year to clinch the Japan SBK title. Doug Polen became synonymous with Ducati when he out-did himself during the Superbike World Championship 1991: Winning 17 out of 26 races, he scored 150 points ahead of second-placed Ducati works rider Raymond Roche. Right after successfully defending his Championship title, he placed second in the AMA Superbike Championship. But Doug Polen wasn't done yet. During the 1994 Superbike Championship, he went on to win third place three times for the UK Honda team.

Super Bilanz für Doug Polen: 27 von 79 Rennen in der Superbike-WM gewonnen. Mehr als jedes dritte Rennen. Klasse. Der 1960 geborene Ex-Motorradrennfahrer ist für viele einer dieser Heroen, die in einer Heldenliste auf keinen Fall fehlen dürfen. Seine Karriere startete er in der amerikanischen Superbike-Meisterschaft (AMA Super-bike Championship) bereits in den frühen Achtziger-jahren – bevor er sich für ein paar Jahre aus dem Rennsport zurückzog. Die Saison 1988 bestritt er auf einer Yoshimura-Suzuki-Werksmaschine, ein Jahr später gewann er die Klassen TT-F1 und TT-F3 bei der japani-schen Motorradmeisterschaft. Dann wurde er Mister Ducati und startete bei der Superbike-Weltmeister-schaft richtig durch: 17 von 26 Rennen gewann Polen und erfuhr sich einen Vorsprung von 150 Punkten vor dem Zweitplatzierten, Ducati-Werkspilot Raymond Roche. Kurz darauf verteidigte er seinen WM-Titel erfolgreich und wurde direkt noch Zweiter in der AMA Superbike Championship. Weil das noch nicht genug war, landete er in der Superbike-WM-Saison 1994 gleich noch dreimal auf den dritten Treppchen für das Honda-UK-Team.

MARCO LUCCHINELLI

He's the wild mustang among wild ponies. The one to burn rubber among those left to idle. The one who steps up among all those who step down. He's Marco Lucchinelli, whose career began on a Laverda and ended on a Ducati—well, not really—after all, he did sign up as Ducati team manager back in 1988, right after his racing career. A career encompassing 13 fast-paced years as a motorcycle racing pro, 82 races, 19 podium places, and 6 MotoGP victories in the 500 cc Championship. Not to mention the hearts of all those fans in his native Italy, which he won over riding on Suzuki, Yamaha, Honda, Cagiva, and Ducati. They used to call him "Crazy Horse" or "Lucky" Lucchinelli.

Er ist das „Crazy Horse" unter den wilden Ponys. Der Rasante unter den Rastenden. Der Aufstehende unter den Fallenden. Marco Lucchinelli. Der, dessen Karriere auf einer Laverda begann und auf einer Ducati endete – wobei, nicht ganz, er ließ sich 1988 direkt im Anschluss an seine aktive Rennfahrerzeit als Ducati-Teammanager verpflichten. Von da an blickt der Italiener zurück auf 13 rasante Jahre als Profifahrer, 82 Rennen, 19 Podiums-plätze und 6 MotoGP-Siege in der Weltmeisterschaft 500-cm³-Klasse. In die Herzen der italienischen Fans fuhr er sich mit Suzuki, Yamaha, Honda, Cagiva und Ducati. Als „Crazy Horse", gerne auch als „Lucky" Lucchinelli.

Panigale is a small suburb of Bologna in Italy. It is where Ducati has spent decades building its motorcycles, striving to do things better, and with even greater precision than the competition. Developed as a successor to the 1198, the 1199 was a total innovation and drew on extensive parts from the race bike division. The 1299 is different again, with a new Superquadro engine with bulked up displacement thanks to a new bore, 205 hp, and 145 Newton meters of torque. The Quick Shift system means that the gears are as fast and precise as on a race bike.

Panigale ist ein kleiner Vorort von Bologna. Ducati baut dort seit Jahrzehnten seine Motorräder mit dem Anspruch, dies besser und präziser zu machen, als die Konkurrenz. Als Nachfolgerin der 1198 war bereits die 1199 eine komplette Neuentwicklung mit zahlreichen Zutaten aus der Rennsportabteilung. Die 1299 kommt jetzt wieder mit neuem Superquadro-Motor, mehr Hubraum dank neuer Bohrung, 205 PS und 145 Newtonmeter Drehmoment. Dank Quick Shift knallen die Gänge dabei so schnell und präzise wie im Rennsport.

TECH SPECS

ENGINE:

L-twin

POWER:

151 kW (205 hp) at 10,500 rpm

DISPLACEMENT:

1,285 cc

DUCATI
Panigale 1299

Ducati's Monster was the original product of necessity. When the budget tide went out in 1992, they turned to the kit principle, resorting to parts from their shelves without further ado. Featuring the frame and chassis from the superbikes, the engine from the supersport shelf, and a simple and minimalist design, Angel Galluzzi created a bike in the tradition of streetfighter machines. The 145-hp 1200 S Stripe now sees the birth of the mightiest power Monster of all time.

Das Monster bei Ducati wurde ursprünglich aus der Not geboren. Denn als 1992 Ebbe in der Haushaltskasse herrschte, bediente man sich kurzerhand nach dem Baukastenprinzip in den eigenen Regalen. Rahmen und Fahrwerk stammen von den Superbikes, der Motor aus dem Supersportregal, das Design simpel und reduziert, gezeichnet von Angel Galluzzi in der Tradition der Streetfighter-Maschinen. Mit der 1200 S Stripe steht aktuell mit 145 PS das stärkste Monster aller Zeiten bereit.

TECH SPECS

ENGINE:

L-twin

POWER:

107 kW (145 hp) at 8,750 rpm

DISPLACEMENT:

1,198 cc

DUCATI
Monster 1200 S Stripe

DUCATI
Streetfighter 848

TECH SPECS

ENGINE:

V2

POWER:

93 kW (132 hp) at 10,000 rpm

DISPLACEMENT:

849 cc

Ducati has made a little fighter, the 848, to stand alongside the big one. Extremely maneuverable and somewhat more comfortable than the Streetfighter 1098, thanks to a different seat and slightly higher handlebars, the little Fighter is aimed at all those who get their kicks on hairpin roads. This machine weighs in at only 372 pounds and is kitted out with an engine that pulls harder than most 1,000-cc bikes, right from the bottom of the rev range.

Dem großen Kämpfer stellt Ducati mit der 848 einen kleineren zur Seite. Extrem handlich und auch aufgrund von veränderter Sitzbank und etwas höherem Lenker etwas komfortabler als die Streetfighter 1098, richtet sich der kleine Fighter direkt an alle, die vor allem auf kurvigen Straßen nach Spaß lechzen. Nur 169 kg leicht und mit einem Motor ausgestattet, der gerade im Drehzahlkeller stärker antritt als die meisten 1000-cm³-Maschinen.

TECH SPECS

DUCATI
Diavel

ENGINE:

V2

POWER:

119 kW (162 hp) at 9,500 rpm

DISPLACEMENT:

1,198 cc

When Italian designers dare to dream, that's a touchstone for the creation of a little beauty like this. Ducati's designers managed to fulfill their dreams and create a muscular silhouette with a 62-inch wheelbase, a curb weight of 516 pounds, and a deep riding position, all powered by a water-cooled 90-degree V2 producing 162 hp. Incidentally, its name is thanks to a Ducati employee who, when he first saw it, thought it looked as "mean as the devil." "Diavel" stands for "devil" in the local Bologna dialect.

Wenn italienische Designer träumen dürfen, dann kommt bisweilen so etwas dabei heraus. So durften sich die Designer bei Ducati selbstverwirklichen und schufen eine muskulöse Silhouette mit 1590 mm Radstand, einem fahrfertigem Gewicht von 234 kg und einer tiefen Sitzposition. Angetrieben wird alles von einem wassergekühlten 90-Grad-V2 mit 162 PS. Ihren Namen verdankt die Diavel übrigens einem Mitarbeiter, der beim Anblick „bösartig wie der Teufel" gedacht hat. „Diavel" bedeutet im Dialekt Bolognas „Teufel".

TECH SPECS

ENGINE:

V2, four-stroke

POWER:

44 kW (60 hp) at 6,200 rpm

DISPLACEMENT:

1,206 CC

PRODUCTION:

1966–1980

HARLEY-DAVIDSON

FLH 1200 Elektra-Glide Shovelhead

Movie classics like *Easy Rider* and *Terminator* notwithstanding, Harley-Davidson is truly renowned for one fine specimen in particular–namely, the E-Glide. In 1966, it was one of the first Harleys to feature an electric starter, hence the affix "Electra." For those ready to travel to the end of the world, this new highway steamboat also came with factory-made cowling, side, and top cases. Harley also responded to market demands for more power and more speed with its advanced Panhead engine design. A modified V2 good for 60 hp, this new power plant was easily recognizable with its unique cylinder heads, which quickly gave this bike its nickname "Shovelhead." Weighing in at 780 pounds, the E-Glide was anything but a lightweight.

Den eigentlichen Ruf von Harley-Davidson begründete – *Easy Rider* hin, *Terminator* her – die Electra-Glide. 1966 eines der ersten Harley-Motorräder mit Elektrostarter, daher auch die Zusatzbezeichnung „Electra". Ab Werk war der neue Highway-Dampfer für alle, die bis ans Ende der Welt reisen wollten, mit Verkleidung, Seitenkoffern und Topcase ausgestattet. Auf das Marktverlangen nach „mehr Power" und „mehr Speed" reagierte Harley mit dem weiterentwickelten Panhead-Motor. Optisch war das modifizierte, nun 60 PS starke V2-Triebwerk an seinen neuen Zylinderköpfen zu erkennen, die ihm gleich den Spitznamen „Shovelhead" einbrachten. Mit mehr als sieben Zentnern war die E-Glide alles andere als ein Leichtgewicht.

Back in the early 1950s, Harley engineers in Milwaukee came up with a new engine design in order to compete in earnest with the likes of BSA, Triumph, and Norton. Harley's new 750-cc V2 design was significantly smaller and lighter than the enormous 1,200-cc and 1,340-cc Big Twins, giving rise to the new Sportster generation in 1952. Always itching to race, many bikers out there liked to tamper with the new bikes, producing outrageously fast 750 Sportsters to race each other with at the dirt track. In response to that new trend, Harley launched the first XL 883 Sportster featuring a new OHV engine in 1957. The following year, Harley really put the petal to the metal with the XLCH 883 Sportster. "CH" stood for "competition hot," and this little Harley was hot, all right. It produced 55 hp and could hit 110 mph with no sweat.

Die Techniker in Milwaukee entwickelten Anfang der Fünfzigerjahre einen neuen Blockmotor, um den Konkurrenten von BSA, Triumph und Norton endlich die Stirn bieten zu können. Das 750er V2-Triebwerk war bedeutend kleiner und leichter als die gewaltigen 1200er und 1340er Big-Twins. Die neue Sportster-Generation war 1952 geboren. Rennverrückte Biker frisierten ihre Maschinen und fuhren mit ihren pfeilschnellen 750er Sportster bei Dirt-Track-Rennen um die Wette. Die Motor Company reagierte und stellte 1957 die erste XL 883 Sportster mit neuem OHV-Motor vor. Ein Jahr später folgte der Hammer: die XLCH 883 Sportster. „CH" bedeutet „competition hot". Und „hot" war die kleine Harley allemal. 55 PS stark und gut 180 Sachen schnell.

TECH SPECS

ENGINE:

V2, four-stroke

POWER:

41 kW (55 hp) at 6,700 rpm

DISPLACEMENT:

883 cc

PRODUCTION:

1958–1971

HARLEY-DAVIDSON
XLCH 883 Sportster

TECH SPECS

HARLEY-DAVIDSON
Softail

ENGINE:

V2, four-stroke

POWER:

41 kW (56 hp) at 5,200 rpm

DISPLACEMENT:

1,338 cc

PRODUCTION:

1984–2000

The year 1984 is a special one in the history of Harley-Davidson in that it marks the company's introduction of its 1,338-cc Evolution engine. In the same vein, it was the introduction of one of the company's milestones, namely the Harley-Davidson Softail. Here was a genuine chopper sporting an extended fork, a thin front wheel, a high handlebar, forward-mounted footrests, 2-up seat, and rigid vintage 40s-style frame. Actually, the Softail not only featured a fat rear wheel but also a cantilever rear suspension system with shock absorbers tucked away under the transmission. Power came from the aforementioned Evo engine, which was directly anchored to the Softail's frame, ensuring a genuine chopper ride as well. Capable of 56 hp, Harley's Evolution power plant set new standards in its class.

Das Jahr 1984 ging mit dem neuen 1340er-Evolution-Triebwerk in die Harley-Davidson-Geschichte ein. Zum Meilenstein für die Motor-Company wurde die Softail. Ein echter Chopper mit langer Gabel, dünnem Vorderrad, Hochlenker, vorverlegten Fußrasten, Stufensitzbank und der Optik eines starren Rahmens aus den Vierzigerjahren. In Wirklichkeit war die Hinterradschwinge mit dem breiten Reifen gefedert, zwei Federbeine lagen flach unter dem Motorblock. Für den Antrieb sorgte besagter Evo-Motor. Um ein kerniges Fahrgefühl zu garantieren, war der Motorblock direkt im Rahmen verschraubt. Das Evolution-Aggregat setzte neue Maßstäbe, seine Leistung lag bei 56 PS.

TECH SPECS

HARLEY-DAVIDSON

XL 1200 X Forty Eight

ENGINE:

V2

POWER:

50 kw (68 hp) at 5,750 rpm

DISPLACEMENT:

1,202 cc

The turn signals house the bike's tail and brake lights so the rear fender is left uncluttered. This model has no passenger seat at all. On a classic single seater the fender has to be exposed—compare this with the "Bobber" tradition since its origins in the customizing scene from the early 1950s. It also has wide tires on spoked wheels and a typical, air-cooled 1,202-cc V2. Riders looking for a cool and more consistent customization can also remove the small fender over the front wheel.

Damit der hintere Fender frei liegen kann, wurden Rück- und Bremsleuchten außen in die Blinker integriert. Einen Soziussitz gibt es erst gar nicht. Beim klassischen Single Seater darf der Fender frei liegen, so wie es die Tradition der Bobber seit ihren Ursprüngen in der Customizing-Szene Anfang der Fünfzigerjahre verlangt. Dazu gibt es dicke Reifen auf Speichenfelgen und einen typischen, luftgekühlten V2 mit 1202 cm³ Hubraum. Wer konsequent ist, entfernt auch noch den kleinen Fender am Vorderrad.

Don't let the name deceive you! "Fat Bob" absolutely does not stand for a comfortable, wide, and heavy V2, ideal for relaxed cruising on endless highways. Quite the opposite: From a Harley-Davidson perspective, the Fat Bob should be regarded as a sports bike. A comparatively short wheelbase and a V2 generating 79 hp ensure fun on those hairpin roads.

Man darf sich vom Namen nicht täuschen lassen: „Fat Bob" steht ganz und gar nicht für einen bequemen, dicken und schweren V2, der zum entspannten Cruisen auf endlosen Highways einlädt. Im Gegenteil: Für eine Harley-Davidson darf die Fat Bob durchaus als sportliches Bike bezeichnet werden. Ein vergleichsweise kurzer Radstand und ein 79 PS starker V2 taugen durchaus für Spaß auf kurvigen Serpentinen.

TECH SPECS

ENGINE:

V2

POWER:

58 kw (79 hp) at 5,010 rpm

DISPLACEMENT:

1,690 cc

HARLEY-DAVIDSON
FXDF Fat Bob

This is it: The mother of all bipedal behemoths! Not only did it look as oversized as a heavily pregnant cow when the so-called sports bike was introduced in 1974, it roughly weighed as much too. Its low center of gravity is supported by the fuel tank, which, by the way, is not the thing you see mounted in front of the seat. The real thing feeding the Gold Wing's 1,000-cc boxer-four is actually located underneath the seat. Rather than surpass its BMW and Moto Guzzi competitors with wings of gold, this big shaft-driven beast ended up staggering behind them at the first sign of fast cornering.

Sie ist die Mutter aller Zweirad-Wohnmobile. 1974 sah die als Sportmaschine vorgestellte Kardan-Bike nicht nur aus wie eine Kuh im neunten Monat, sondern wog auch etwa so viel. Tief der Schwerpunkt vom neuen Vierzylinder-Boxermotor, unterstützt vom Tank, der in Wahrheit eine Attrappe war. Der Kraftstoff für den 1000er-Triebsatz wurde unter der Sitzbank gebunkert. Die Wuchtbrumme sollte die Konkurrenz von BMW und Moto Guzzi golden überflügeln, geriet aber bei sportlicher Fahrweise eher ins Schwimmen.

TECH SPECS

ENGINE:

Four-cylinder boxer, four-stroke

POWER:

61 kW (82 hp) at 7,000 rpm

DISPLACEMENT:

999 CC

PRODUCTION:

1974–1978

HONDA
Gold Wing GL 1000

TECH SPECS

ENGINE:

Four-cylinder in-line, four-stroke

POWER:

50 kW (67 hp) at 8,000 rpm

DISPLACEMENT:

736 CC

PRODUCTION:

1969–1978

HONDA
CB 750 Four

By the mid-1960s, Hondas were running circles around competitors all over the world, dominating world championship racing in all five classes. Honda had become a household name in motorcycle racing and toward the end of the decade the company decided now was the time to introduce a big and powerful bike. Sure enough, in the space of just one-and-a-half years, Honda designers produced what was initially called the "Honda Four." The 750-cc Four went on to become the first mass-produced motorbike to feature an in-line four power plant, delivering 67 hp while topping 125 mph. What made this power plant all the more sensational was its overall reliability, as it proved virtually indestructible. It just kept going and going, making the Four the darling of a young and motorcycle-craving generation. Indeed, in 1999, the Honda CB 750 Four was named Motorcycle of the Century by motorcycle fans from all over the world.

Bis Mitte der Sechzigerjahre kreisten die Honda-Werksmaschinen konkurrenzlos in allen WM-Klassen über die Rennpisten der Welt. Der Name Honda war in aller Munde und das Ende des Jahrzehnts genau der richtige Zeitpunkt, um ein großes, leistungsstarkes Motorrad auf den Markt zu bringen. In nur eineinhalb Jahren stellte die Entwicklungsabteilung die „Honda Four", wie sie anfangs hieß, auf die Räder. Die 750er-Four war das erste in Großserie gebaute Motorrad mit Vierzylinder-Reihenmotor, 67 PS stark und 200 km/h schnell. Die nächste Sensation war die Zuverlässigkeit: Der Motor war nicht kaputt zu kriegen, die Four lief und lief und wurde so zum Liebling einer jungen, motorradverrückten Generation. 1999 kürten Fans aus der weltweiten Szene die Honda CB 750 Four zum Motorrad des Jahrhunderts.

TECH SPECS

ENGINE:

Four-cylinder in-line, four-stroke

POWER:

63 kW (85 hp) at 12,000 rpm

DISPLACEMENT:

600 cc

PRODUCTION:

1986–1993

HONDA
CBR 600 F

Did you know that the 1980s weren't nearly as straight-laced as they seemed? Apparently, neither did Honda when they clad the CBR 600 F to the point where it didn't reveal the slightest clue about its inner mechanics to the outside world. Which is too bad, since the engine of this fully clad bike offered plenty to behold, especially in terms of its capacity. Boasting 600 cc, it was an outright challenge to the competition. Add to that 85 hp, two overlying camshafts, 16 valves, and liquid cooling, and you had a combination that could effortlessly propel this Honda to a top speed of 145 mph.

In den Achtzigerjahren ging es alles andere als prüde zu. Und doch verhüllte Honda ihre CBR 600 F auf eine Weise, die äußerlich keinen Rückschluss auf das mechanisierte Innenleben zuließ. Dabei konnte sich das neue 600er-Triebwerk des vollverkleideten Mittelklasse-Sportlers allein aufgrund seines Hubraums sehen lassen. In der 600er-Supersport-Klasse bedeutete dies eine klare Kampfansage. 85 PS, zwei obenliegende Nockenwellen, 16 Ventile und die Flüssigkeitskühlung waren in dieser Klasse richtungsweisend und trugen ihren Teil dazu bei, dass die CBR 600 F locker 230 km/h Spitze schaffte.

Chief developer Baba-san created a new sports bike. Picture a motorcycle, stripped to its bare essentials with only a minimum number of parts needed to assemble it—this is what Honda must've pictured in 1992 when they launched the 900-cc Fireblade. With its lean, no-frills body design and lightweight construction, it barely weighed 440 pounds at a time when other super sport bikes weighed in at an additional 100 pounds. The difference in handling was undeniable: The "Blade," as it was called by enthusiasts, launched like a bat out of hell once you opened the throttle and yet maintained firm contact with the pavement, exhibited quick, razor-sharp cornering, stopped on a dime, and actually left the driver in control at all times.

Chef-Entwickler Baba-san kreierte ein neues Sportmotorrad, lässt alles Überflüssige weg und baut den Rest mit möglichst wenig Einzelteilen. Das Ergebnis: Honda kommt 1992 mit der 900er-Fireblade auf den Markt. Schlank, konsequent in der Linienführung, leicht im Bau, gerade mal gute 200 kg schwer. Die Konkurrenz im Supersportsektor wog zu der Zeit noch über einen Zentner mehr. Was sich auf die Fahreigenschaften auswirkte: Die „Blade", wie sie Honda-Fans nannten, nahm giftig das Gas an und hielt straff den Kontakt zum Asphalt, huschte flink um die Ecken und blieb dennoch in der Spur, bremste kräftig und überließ dem Fahrer jederzeit die Kontrolle.

TECH SPECS

ENGINE:

Four-cylinder, in-line four-stroke

POWER:

93 kW (126 hp) at 10,000 rpm

DISPLACEMENT:

893 cc

PRODUCTION:

1992–1999

HONDA
CBR 900 RR Fireblade

Launched in 1985, the VFR 750 F was another superb motorbike made by Honda: With a new water-cooled four-stroke V4, it was nimble, reliable, and high-performance too. As such, it had all the right stuff for the popular superbike championships. That's because its roots traced directly back to another high-performance motorbike made affordable for everyone. Against this backdrop, Honda chose the street-version VFR 750 F as the basis for developing a purely bred sports version called the VFR 750 R, or RC 30 for short. Launched just in time for the recently organized Superbike World Championship of 1988, the RC 30 equally made its appearance as a street-legal superbike at Honda dealerships and as a factory-tuned race bike ready at the start line out on the racetrack. It was a high-performance motorbike that excelled with its fantastic handling, superb road-holding characteristics, and a high-tech engine that delivered irresistible driving dynamics. In fact, an RC 30 helped its driver Helmut Dähne set a new lap record for street bikes at 7:49.71 minutes at Germany's Nürburgring-Nordschleife back in 1993, a lap record which has yet to be broken. No doubt, the RC 30 is the King of the Ring.

Mit der VFR 750 F gelang Honda 1985 ein Motorrad mit neuem wassergekühltem V4-Viertakt-Triebwerk: flink, zuverlässig, mit hohen Laufleistungen. Gleichzeitig auch die ideale Rennvorlage für die populäre Superbike-Meisterschaft. Voraussetzung für die Teilnahme war nämlich die direkte Abstammung von einem für jedermann käuflichen Sportmotorrad. Und so entwickelte Honda aus der zivilen VFR 750 F das reinrassige Sportgerät VFR 750 R, kurz RC 30. Pünktlich für die neu geschaffene Superbike-WM 1988 stand die RC 30 als zulassungsfähiges Straßen-Superbike in den Honda-Verkaufsräumen und mit Werkskit getunt am Start auf der Piste. Eine Sportmaschine mit tollem Handling, bestechender Straßenlage und einem High-Tech-Motor, der eine fantastische Fahrdynamik lieferte. Eine RC 30 trug Helmut Dähne 1993 zum bis heute gültigen Rundenrekord für straßenzugelassene Bikes auf der Nürburgring-Nordschleife. 7:49,71 Minuten. King of the Ring.

TECH SPECS

ENGINE:

V4, four-stroke

POWER:

83 kW (112 hp) at 9,500 rpm

DISPLACEMENT:

748 cc

PRODUCTION:

1987–1992

HONDA
VFR 750 R (RC 30)

TECH SPECS

ENGINE:

Four-cylinder in-line, four-stroke

POWER:

70 kW (95 hp) at 9,000 rpm

DISPLACEMENT:

895 cc

PRODUCTION:

1978–1984

The CB 900 F proved an absolute hit and not just on the street. In the sports segment of the late 1970s, no other bike outsold it. European versions of this sport touring chrome-and-aluminum clad machine bore the notable byname "Bol d'Or," an homage to the famous 24-hour endurance race where Honda regularly slaughtered the competition between 1976 and 1978. With the CB 900 F Bol d'Or, customers now came into possession of the same performance-tested technology. Its in-line four-stroke with two overhead camshafts and four-valve cylinder heads was capable of 95 hp, propelling this superbike to its top speed of 132 mph with almost terrifying ease.

Die CB 900 F entpuppte sich nicht nur auf der Straße als absoluter Renner. Im Sportsegment verkaufte sich Ende der Siebzigerjahre kein anderes Modell erfolgreicher als die 900er-Honda. Auf dem europäischen Markt wurde der Supersportler mit dem Zusatzlogo „Bol d'Or" geadelt. Eine Ehrung für die Erfolge beim berühmtesten 24-Stunden-Langstreckenrennen der Welt, der Bol d'Or in Frankreich. Von 1976 bis 1978 hatten die Honda-Werksteams bei diesem Marathon die Konkurrenz regelrecht versägt. Mit der CB 900 F Bol d'Or kam die Kundschaft nun in Besitz der im Rennsport bewährten Technologie. Der Vierzylinder-Motor mit zwei obenliegenden Nockenwellen und vier Ventilen pro Zylinder leistete 95 PS. Genug Power für 220 Sachen.

HONDA
CB 900 F *(Bol d'Or)*

"King of the Roads" isn't a distinction that's easily earned. Unless you eat insanity for breakfast or you have a history of winning the Isle of Man Tourist Trophy 26 times. Or both. Most of all, you'd have to be as capable of riding a bullet bike as Joey Dunlop. And this is bound to be the hard part, considering that Dunlop, a native of Ireland, is regarded as one of the best motor racing pros ever. He started in 98 races, clinching trophies in 80 of them. His track record shows 250 rounds completed at average speeds north of 112 mph. The fastest he ever went through any round was 124 mph in the year 2000, which, sadly, would also prove to be his last. That year, Dunlop fatally crashed during a race he had helped sponsor on Pirita-Kose-Kloostrimetsa Circuit in Tallinn, Estonia. Joey Dunlop remains unforgotten not only by his five children, but also by visitors to the Isle of Man. Here, a section of the TT course was named after him—and a statue was erected in his memory. Naturally, the statue is of Joey astride a Honda.

„King of the Roads" wird man nicht einfach so. Dafür muss man entweder eine Portion Wahnsinn gefrühstückt oder 26 Mal die Isle of Man Tourist Trophy gewonnen haben. Oder beides. Hauptsache, man beherrscht den Ritt auf einer Kanonenkugel wie Joey Dunlop. Und das könnte schwierig werden, schließlich gilt der Ire als einer der besten Straßenrennfahrer der Geschichte. 98 Mal startete er bei Rennen, 80 Preise gewann er. Mehr als 250 Runden absolvierte er mit durchschnittlich mehr als 180 Sachen. Seine schnellste Runde fuhr Dunlop mit 199,34 km/h in dem Jahr, das sein letztes sein sollte: 2000. Und das Letzte was er getan hat war: Rennen fahren. Er verunglückte bei einem von ihm selbst unterstützen Rennen auf dem Pirita-Kose-Kloostrimetsa in Tallinn. Unvergessen bleibt Dunlop nicht nur für seine fünf Kinder, sondern auch für die Isle-of-Man-Besucher. Ein Streckenabschnitt wurde nach ihm benannt – eine Statue errichtet. Zu sehen: Klar, Joey auf einem Bike.

JOEY DUNLOP

THE BIKES – OUR HEROES · IRELAND

With five consecutive 500 cc World Championships, Mick Doohan (or should we call him "Mister Honda?") has really outdone himself. But let's start from the beginning: During the 1994 season, he outraced everyone in 9 out of 14 races, defending his Championship title the following year. In 1996, he clinched his third consecutive title, riding his way to podium places in 12 out of 15 races. It was in 1997 and 1998 when Doohan outdid himself by clinching his forth and fifth title in the 500 cc World Championship. He retired only one year later, though, after suffering a series of leg injuries. But it's his incredible track record his fans remember him for: 54 victories in the Motorcycle World Championship, 95 podium places, 58 pole positions, and 46 of the fastest laps measured. The native of Australia also became the first motorcycle racer to be inducted into the MotoGP Hall of Fame. From 2000 until 2004, Doohan worked as team manager for Honda Racing Corporation, where he landed another coup when he insisted that his potential successor on the racetrack be none other than Valentino Rossi.

Mick Doohan, nennen wir ihn „Mister Honda", hat es geschafft, sich mit fünf Weltmeistertiteln in Folge selbst die Krone aufzusetzen. Der Reihe nach: In der Saison 1994 fuhr er bei 9 von 14 Rennen alle anderen in Grund und Boden, im Jahr darauf verteidigte er seinen Weltmeistertitel. 1996 holte er seinen dritten Titel in Folge und fuhr in 12 von 15 Rennen aufs Podium. 1997 und 1998 übertraf sich Doohan selbst und holte seinen vierten und fünften Titel in der 500-cm³-Königsklasse. Schon ein Jahr später trat er zurück, nachdem er sich das Bein zum wiederholten Male schwer verletzte. Er ist seinen Fans mit einer unglaublichen Bilanz in Erinnerung geblieben: 54 Siege in der Motorrad-WM, 95 Podiumsplätze, 58 Polepositions, 46 schnellste Rennrunden. Der Australier wurde als erster Motorradrennfahrer in die MotoGP Hall of Fame aufgenommen. Von 2000 bis 2004 arbeitete er als Teammanager bei der Honda Racing Corporation. Und landete in dieser Funktion seinen nächsten Coup, indem er keinen Geringeren als Valentino Rossi als potenziellen Nachfolgefahrer verpflichten ließ.

 # MICK DOOHAN

TECH SPECS

HONDA
CBR 300 R

ENGINE:

Single-cylinder

POWER:

23 kW (31 hp) at 8,500 rpm

DISPLACEMENT:

286 cc

More displacement for this lightweight sports bike is Honda's philosophy for pushing the smallest race bike in the CBR family. This model has 286 cc, that's 37 cc more than its predecessor, to give it 31 hp. The increased capacity was achieved by lengthening the stroke of the single-cylinder engine, which can now give more than 70 mpg. Furthermore, the successor to the CBR 250 R is now more clearly aligned with the top of the range supersport model, the CBR 1000 RR Fireblade.

Mehr Hubraum für das Leichtgewicht unter den Sportlern. Mit dieser Philosophie pusht Honda seine kleinste Rennmaschine der CBR-Familie. 286 cm³ Hubraum, und damit 37 cm³ mehr als bei der Vorgängerin, verhelfen ab diesem Modelljahr zu 31 PS. Erreicht wird der Volumenzuwachs durch einen verlängerten Hub des Einzylinders, der jetzt mit einem Liter Benzin mehr als 30 Kilometer zurücklegen können soll. Äußerlich orientiert sich die Nachfolgerin der CBR 250 R jetzt deutlich stärker am Supersport-Topmodell CBR 1000 RR Fireblade.

TECH SPECS

ENGINE:

V4

POWER:

133 kW (181 hp) at 12,250 rpm

DISPLACEMENT:

999 CC

HONDA
CBR 1000 RR Fireblade

With five Isle of Man TT race wins under its belt, the Fireblade has achieved legendary status. In fact, at its launch in 1992, it supremely defined the super-sports category: Consistent weight reductions and performance that have yet to be matched by any other production motorcycle. To this day, the Japanese have upheld this tradition. This model now has 999 cc and 181 hp and with aerodynamics borrowed straight from the race circuit.

Mit fünf Siegen bei der Tourist Trophy auf der Isle of Man schaffte sich die Fireblade einen Legendenstatus. Und durch die Tatsache, dass sie bei ihrer Einführung 1992 die Kategorie der Supersportler im Grunde definiert hat: Konsequente Gewichtsreduzierung und Fahrleistungen, die so bis dato von keinem anderen Serienmotorrad erreicht wurden. Diese Tradition pflegen die Japaner bis heute. Mittlerweile mit 999 cm³ Hubraum und 181 PS. Die Aerodynamik wurde direkt beim Rennsport entliehen.

From time to time, it's worth coming out with a clear statement for edgy design. That's exactly what Honda did with the NM 4 Vultus: A bike with a sci-fi look as a Hollywood film designer might have imagined it. These edgy features conceal the chassis and engine taken from Honda's NC range. In real terms, this means a twin-cylinder engine with 55 hp and 68 Newton meters of torque, coupled to an electronically controlled dual-clutch gearbox, which can also be used manually.

Bisweilen gilt es, eindeutig Stellung zu beziehen und Ecken und Kanten zu zeigen. Mit der NM 4 Vultus macht Honda genau das. Ein Bike mit einer Science-Fiction-Optik, die so auch einem Filmdesigner in Hollywood hätte einfallen können. Technisch stecken unter diesen Kanten Fahrwerk und Antrieb aus Hondas NC-Baureihe. Konkret heißt das: ein Zweizylinder mit 55 PS und 68 Newtonmeter Drehmoment, die Schaltarbeit übernimmt ein elektrisch gesteuertes Doppelkupplungs-getriebe, das auch den manuellen Eingriff erlaubt.

TECH SPECS

ENGINE:

V2

POWER:

40 kW (55 hp) at 6,250 rpm

DISPLACEMENT:

745 cc

HONDA
NM 4 Vultus

The spiritual roots are across the pond in the US, and this cross between a cruiser and tourer motorcycle inspired the CTX model made in Japan. The Japanese know how a "bagger" with handlebar-mount fairing and short windshield works, as the Gold Wing's powerful sister—the F6B—already demonstrated in 2013. Now, the four-cylinder CTX 1300 tourer, with 106 Newton meters of torque and exceptional performance is available to close the gap between the six-cylinder flagship and the considerably smaller CTX 700 with parallel-twin engine.

Die geistigen Wurzeln dieses Cruiser-Tourer-Hybrid liegen in Amerika. Nach dortigem Vorbild wurde die CTX entwickelt, gebaut wird sie in Japan. Dass sie dort wissen, wie eine Bagger mit Lenkverkleidung und ge-kapptem Windschild funktioniert, zeigte bereits 2013 die mächtige Gold-Wing-Schwester F6B. Der Vierzylinder-Flanierer CTX 1300 schließt jetzt mit 106 Newtonmetern Drehmoment und souveränen Fahrleistungen die Lücke zwischen dem Sechszylinder-Flagschiff und der deutlich kleineren CTX 700 mit Reihen-Twin.

TECH SPECS

ENGINE:

V4

POWER:

62 kW (84 hp) at 6,000 rpm

DISPLACEMENT:

1,261 cc

HONDA
CTX 1300

TECH SPECS

ENGINE:

V2

POWER:

72 kW (100 hp) at 8,000 rpm

DISPLACEMENT:

1,811 cc

INDIAN MOTORCYCLES
Indian Roadmaster

Hop on and get going—with a passenger, if you prefer—until an empty tank brings you to a halt. When it comes down to it, that's the philosophy of Indian Motorcycles. Indian pays due respect to this philosophy with its Roadmaster: 37 gallons of storage space, protected from the weather, great leg room, adjustable passenger footboards, three 12-V sockets, electronic cruise control, a vast array of infotainment and drive provided by the well-known Thunder Stroke 111, an air-cooled 49-degree V2 engine with six-speed gearbox, and overdrive function.

Aufsitzen und losfahren – gerne auch zu zweit – so lange bis der leere Tank zum Anhalten zwingt. Im Kern ist genau das die Philosophie von Indian Motorcycles. Und mit der Roadmaster zollt Indian dieser Philosophie den nötigen Respekt: wettergeschützter Stauraum mit 143 Litern Fassungsvermögen, großzügiger Beinraum, verstellbare Sozius-Trittbretter, drei 12-V-Steckdosen, elektronischer Tempomat, umfangreiches Infotainment-System. Für den Antrieb sorgt der bekannte Thunder Stroke 111, ein luftgekühlter 49-Grad-V2 mit Sechsganggetriebe und Overdrive-Funktion.

INDIAN MOTORCYCLES
Indian Scout

TECH SPECS

ENGINE:

V2

POWER:

72 kW (100 hp) at 8,000 rpm

DISPLACEMENT:

1,133 cc

If you've ever wondered how good-looking a sporty Indian motorcycle might be, the Scout is your answer. Because this liquid-cooled American V2 has thoroughly earned that description. After the comeback of the Chief series, the Scout now aims to capture the medium, open cruiser segment. It's making an entrance here with a much livelier engine, lower weight, and more agile chassis than the Chief models. While its reduced styling with open-bottom frame supporting the 1,133-cc engine targets a much younger buyer, with its 100-hp engine, by a long shot, the Scout is not just regarded as an entry-level machine. Actually, this is a new model range within the Indian family.

Wer sich die Frage stellt, wie wohl eine sportliche Indian aussehen mag, der bekommt mit der Scout die Antwort geliefert. Denn das Attribut „sportlich" hat der flüssigkeitsgekühlte Ami-V2 durchaus verdient. Nach dem Comeback der Chief-Baureihe will die Scout jetzt das Segment der mittleren, unverkleideten Cruiser erobern und tritt hier mit einem deutlich drehfreudigeren Motor, geringerem Gewicht und agilerem Fahrwerk an als die Chief-Modelle. Auch wenn sich das reduzierte Styling mit einem nach unten offenen Rahmen, der den 1133-cm³-Motor trägt, an eine deutlich jüngere Käuferschaft richtet, gilt die Scout mit ihren 100 PS bei Weitem nicht einfach als Einsteigermaschine, sondern ist tatsächlich eine neue Modellreihe innerhalb der Indian-Familie.

KAWASAKI

500 H1 Mach III

TECH SPECS

ENGINE:

Three-cylinder in-line, two-stroke

POWER:

44 kW (60 hp) at 8,500 rpm

DISPLACEMENT:

498 CC

PRODUCTION:

1969–1977

When it came to speed and acceleration, few motorcycles could keep up with the Mach III. Hitting the quarter mile in less than 13 seconds and reaching a top speed of 120 mph, the Kawasaki 500 H1 was one of the fastest factory-made rides in the late 1960s. But performance wasn't its only asset. Its benign handling characteristics and top sound equally made it a winner among motorcyclists. The top-of-the-line 500 H1 boasted three carbs and, like its predecessor, three exhaust pipes. The showstopper 500 model also came equipped with a newly designed air-cooled three-cylinder two-stroke power plant. Unfortunately, road handling and stability of the 500 H1 proved abysmal. Testers in the U.S. had a royal fit over it.

Wenn es Ende der Sechzigerjahre um Beschleunigung und Geschwindigkeit ging, konnte kein Motorrad mit der Mach III mithalten. Die Viertelmeile schluckte sie in weniger als 13 Sekunden weg, ruckzuck zeigte die Tachonadel 200 an. Die Kawasaki 500 H1 war damals eines der schnellsten Serienmotorräder der Welt. Dabei überzeugte sie in erster Linie mit höllischer Leistung und grellem Sound. Ausgestattet war das 500er-Vorzeigebike mit einem neu entwickelten luftgekühlten Drei-Zylinder-Zweitakt-Triebwerk. Handling und Spurstabilität waren dagegen die reinste Katastrophe. In den USA rasteten die Tester schier aus. Sie schrieben von „unbändiger Kraft" und bezeichneten sie als „Rodeo-Bike".

TECH SPECS

ENGINE:

Three-cylinder in-line, two-stroke

POWER:

53 kW (71 hp) at 6,500 rpm

DISPLACEMENT:

748 CC

PRODUCTION:

1971–1975

KAWASAKI

750 H2 Mach IV

As the 1960s drew to a close, the Kawasaki 500 H1 Mach III was deemed the ultimate rodeo bike. Then, in 1971, Kawasaki upped the ante by launching the zenith of their three-cylinder two-stroke models: The 750 H2 Mach IV, capable of 71 hp and a top speed north of 125 mph. With opinions clashing over the benefits of two-stroke vs. four-stroke, Yamaha, Suzuki, Honda, and Kawasaki all swore by two-stroke technology. For their part, Kawasaki stringently stuck with it for the 750 H2 in pursuit of their corporate quest to be better, stronger, and faster than the rest. The bar was raised even higher than with the 500 H1 Mach III as the aggressive powerhouse of the 500 gave way to the 750's power unit, whose performance was nothing short of incredible. Whereas the Mach III came to be known as Kawasaki's "rodeo bike," the Mach IV became the proverbial "wolf in sheep's clothing."

Ende der Sechzigerjahre galt die Kawasaki 500 H1 Mach III als „Rodeo-Bike". Die Steigerung und zugleich Krönung in der Dreizylinder-Zweitakt-Baureihe stand ab 1971 als 71 PS starke und mehr als 200 Sachen schnelle 750 H2 Mach IV bei den Händlern. Während noch der Glaubenskrieg Zweitakter oder Viertakter gekämpft wurde, schworen Yamaha, Suzuki und Kawasaki weiterhin auf die agile Zweitakt-Technik. Und auch mit dem 750er-Bike blieb Kawasaki der Unternehmensphilosophie treu: besser, stärker und schneller als alle anderen. Im Vergleich zur 500er Mach III verfügte der neue 750er-Motor über Durchzugskraft und Laufkultur – Zuverlässigkeit und Fahrverhalten konnten sich sehen lassen. Die Mach III blieb das „Rodeo-Bike", die Mach IV verkörperte den „Wolf im Schafspelz".

KAWASAKI
250 S1 Mach I

TECH SPECS

ENGINE:

Three-cylinder in-line, two-stroke

POWER:

21 kW (28 hp) at 7,500 rpm

DISPLACEMENT:

249 cc

PRODUCTION:

1971–1976

Between 1971 and 1974, two-stroke enthusiasts finally had the choice of four Kawasaki two-stroke rides with three-cylinder engines—the 250 S1, the 350 S2, the 500 H1, and the 750 H2. The smallest one of the bunch was the S1 Mach I with a 250-cc engine. Boasting 28 hp at 7,500 rpm, it was similar in design to that of the 500 Mach III. Aside from annual upgrades, this 249-cc two-stroke, ideal for newbies, carried over virtually unchanged as part of the lineup until 1976.

Ab den Modelljahren 1971 und 1974 konnten Kawasaki-Zweitaktfans zwischen fünf Dreizylinder-Maschinen wählen: 250 S1, 350 S2, 400 S4, 500 H1 und 750 H2. Die kleinste im Bunde war ab 1971 die S1 Mach I. Das 250er-Triebwerk leistete 28 PS bei 7500 U/min und entsprach dem konstruktiven Aufbau des 500er-Motors. Abgesehen von der jährlichen Modellpflege, blieb der ideal für Fahranfänger geeignete Viertelliter-Zweitakter bis 1976 unverändert im Programm.

TECH SPECS

ENGINE:

Four-cylinder in-line, four-stroke

POWER:

58 kW (79 hp) at 8,500 rpm

DISPLACEMENT:

903 cc

PRODUCTION:

1972–1976

KAWASAKI
900 Z1

By the end of the 1960s, Kawasaki found itself in a bit of a tight spot. The reason for that was its competitor Honda, which knocked it out of the park when it launched its 750 four-cylinder in 1969. At that time, Kawasaki had been secretly working on its own 750-cc four-cylinder bike version when corporate managers abruptly put the project on hold. Breaking with an internal agreement among Japanese manufacturers to cap their motorcycle output at 750 cc, Kawasaki decided it was time to put the petal to the metal. By launching the 900-cc four-cylinder Z1, the motorcycle maker opened a new chapter in the industry in 1972. After the CB 750 Four, the 900 Z1 became a second milestone in motorcycle history. Producing 79 hp, the Z1 was not without its controversy. As awesome as its four-cylinder power plant was, the suspension of the Z1 came with a whole range of teething problems. Among them was the Z1's tendency to shake so violently at high speeds it could scare the bejesus out of the toughest of riders.

Irgendwie fühlte sich Kawasaki Ende der Sechzigerjahre vor den Kopf gestoßen. Den Grund hierfür lieferte der Konkurrent Honda, der 1969 die CB 750 Four auf den Markt brachte und damit einen Coup landete. Insgeheim entwickelte Kawasaki ebenfalls eine 750er-Vierzylinder-Maschine. Nun stoppten die Manager das Vorhaben. Entgegen interner Absprache unter den japanischen Herstellern, keine Motorräder über 750 Kubik zu bauen, langte Kawasaki nun mächtig zu. Mit dem 900er-Vierzylinder-Big-Bike Z1 schlug das Werk 1972 ein neues Kapitel auf. Nach der CB 750 Four wurde die 900 Z1 zum zweiten Meilenstein in der Motorradgeschichte. Unumstritten war die 79 PS starke Z1 jedoch nicht. Der Vierzylinder-Motor war eine Wucht, das Fahrwerk hatte allerdings noch etliche Kinderkrankheiten. Der Feuerstuhl wackelte bei flottem Tempo so furchtbar, dass selbst den abgebrühtesten Heizern Angst und Bange werden konnte.

TECH SPECS

KAWASAKI

GPZ 900 R NINJA

ENGINE:

Four-cylinder in-line, four-stroke

POWER:

85 kW (115 hp) at 9,600 rpm

DISPLACEMENT:

908 cc

PRODUCTION:

1984–1986

In 1984, Kawasaki was predicted to open a new chapter in company history when it introduced the GPZ 9000 R Ninja. Here was a high-performance motorbike brimming with innovation, not the least of which was its newly designed, liquid-cooled 16-valve DOHC four-cylinder power plant. Boasting 115 hp under its quasi real racing cowl, the Ninja was easily capable of hitting 155 mph. Its suspension, complete with a 16-inch front wheel, not only made for impressive handling characteristics, but fantastic track stability as well. The anti-dive system in the front fork was a flop, however, the idea behind this engineering gimmick being to prevent suspension dive under braking. That was the extent of its criticism, though. With the 900 R Ninja, Kawasaki once again proved better, stronger, and faster than all others.

Erwartungsgemäß schlug Kawasaki 1984 mit der GPZ 9000 R Ninja ein neues Firmenkapitel auf. Der Supersportler strotzte mit dem neu entwickelten, wassergekühlten DOHC-Vierzylinder-Motor mit vier Ventilen pro Brennraum nur so vor Innovation. Mit 115 PS, versteckt unter einer fast echten Rennverkleidung, rannte die Ninja gut 250 Sachen. Das Fahrwerk, mit einem 16-Zoll-Vorderrad ausgestattet, zeigte sich beeindruckend handlich, verfügte aber gleichzeitig über eine bestechende Spurstabilität. Zum Flop wurde dagegen das Anti-Dive-System in der Vordergabel. Mit diesem technischen Gimmick wollten die Techniker beim kräftigen Bremsen mit dem Vorderrad das tiefe Gabeleintauchen verhindern. Das war's aber auch schon mit der Kritik. Wieder einmal war Kawasaki mit der 900er-Ninja besser, stärker und schneller als alle anderen.

GPZ900R
DOHC 16-VALVE

For decades, the name "Ninja" has stood for extremely fast representatives of the Kawasaki family and is practically considered as a brand itself. Interestingly, the addition of the H2 is a reference for enthusiasts, namely to the Mach IV H2. This caused a furor in its day due to its incredible acceleration. Like the ZX-10R, the Ninja H2 comes with 200 hp, but generates 133 Newton meters of torque at 10,500 revs, while the ZX-10R only delivers 112 Newton meters at 13,000 rpm. As if that's not enough, then there's the H2 with the extra "R." The add-on letter as good as means classic Ninja heritage. Thanks to its compressor technology, the H2R achieves 300 hp—so, an acceleration that inevitably recalls memories of the legendary Mach IV H2.

Der Begriff „Ninja" steht seit Jahrzehnten für extrem schnelle Vertreter der Kawasaki-Familie und gilt selbst fast schon als Marke. Der interessante Zusatz H2 ist ein Verweis für Kenner: Er bezieht sich nämlich auf die Mach IV H2, die seinerzeit mit ihrer unglaublichen Beschleunigung für Furore sorgte. Die Ninja H2 kommt wie die ZX-10R mit 200 PS, daher generiert aber 133 Newtonmeter Drehmoment bei 10.500 Touren, während es die ZX-10R „nur" auf 112 Newtonmeter bei 13.000 Umdrehungen bringt. Wem das „zu wenig" ist, für den steht die H2 mit dem Zusatz R bereit. Und dieses „R" ist ein ähnlich gelernter Begriff wie Ninja. Dank Kompressor-Technologie kommt die H2R auf 300 PS – und damit auf eine Beschleunigung, die unweigerlich Erinnerungen an die legendäre Mach IV H2 hervorruft.

TECH SPECS

ENGINE:

V4 or V4 with compressor

POWER:

147 kW (200 hp) or 228 kW (310 hp)

at 11,000 rpm or 14,000 rpm

DISPLACEMENT:

998 cc

KAWASAKI
Ninja H2/H2R

TECH SPECS

ENGINE:

V2

POWER:

37 kW (50 hp) at 5,700 rpm

DISPLACEMENT:

903 CC

KAWASAKI
VN 900 Custom

A chopper—now, that's always meant meeting certain criteria: Low seating position, long fork, and an engine that isn't too quiet and with just the right amount of vibration. The VN 900 Custom does exactly that. With a water-cooled 900-cc four-valve engine, a 21-inch front wheel sitting majestically at the end of the long fork, and a visual rigid-frame of the chassis, this package even provides a supremely comfortable ride in this class as well. To go this far, and yet to expect radically different settings for the chassis—now, that would be asking too much.

Ein Chopper muss seit jeher gewisse Kriterien erfüllen: tiefe Sitzposition, lange Gabel und ein Motor, der nicht zu ruhig läuft und gerade richtig vibriert. Die VN 900 Custom erfüllt genau diese Kriterien. Sie ist ein 900er-Vierventiler, wassergekühlt, an der langen Gabel thront vorne ein 21-Zoll-Vorderrad, und zusammen mit einem Fahrwerk mit Starrahmen-Optik bietet dieses Paket zudem sogar noch sehr guten Fahrkomfort in dieser Klasse. So weit zu gehen und hier gar verschiedene Einstellungsmöglichkeiten für das Fahrwerk zu verlangen, wäre aber zu viel des Guten.

TECH SPECS

ENGINE:

Four-cylinder in-line

POWER:

114 kW (155 hp) at 8,800 rpm

DISPLACEMENT:

1,352 cc

KAWASAKI
1400 GTR

The previous model update was a few years ago, but now the GTR has proven itself. The rather small ZZR 1400 engine guarantees forward propulsion in any given situation. As far as touring qualities go, since 2010, Kawasaki has been relying on a traction control system that can be switched off, heated grips, and tire pressure monitoring, keyless ignition, panniers, luggage carrier, storage compartment, and electric windshield. Added to that are the ABS and a combi brake system, plus brake assist, which also identifies emergency braking and adapts accordingly. Also adjustable is the intensity of the foot brake's effect on the front wheel.

Die letzte Modellpflege ist schon einige Jahre her, doch die GTR hat sich bewährt. Für Vortrieb in jeder Lage sorgt der etwas reduzierte Motor aus der ZZR 1400, und was die Tourerqualitäten angeht, so vertraut die Kawasaki seit 2010 auf eine abschaltbare Traktionskontrolle, Heizgriffe und Reifendruckkontrolle, Keyless-Go, Koffer, Gepäckträger, Ablagefach und elektrisch verstellbare Scheibe. Dazu gibt es ABS und Kombibremse sowie einen Bremsassistenten, der auch Notbremsungen erkennt und entsprechend nachregelt. Die Wirkung der Fußbremse kann zudem in ihrer Intensität auf das Vorderrad eingestellt werden.

TECH SPECS

ENGINE:

Two-cylinder

POWER:

52 kW (70 hp) at 7,200 rpm

DISPLACEMENT:

744 cc

PRODUCTION:

1972–1976

LAVERDA
750 SFC

Its brakes were applied 3,274 times; its gears were shifted 22,353 times—all in just 24 hours. The year was 1971 when the Laverda 750 SFC, running an average speed of 77.85 mph, won the 24 Hours of Oss in the Netherlands. In plain English: It ran circles around anything Triumph, Honda, Suzuki, Kawasaki, and Ducati had to offer. This two-cylinder cult bike was based on the Laverda 750 street bike, although considerably redesigned. It had a powerful parallel-two delivering 70 hp and boosting it to a top speed of 140 mph. Company bosses at Laverda figured if it's good enough for the racetrack, it's good enough for the streets. And, sure enough, Laverda's race bike made its way to showroom floors unchanged as the 750 SFC in 1972.

3274-mal bremsen, 22.353-mal schalten – und das alles an einem Tag am Stück. Es war im Jahr 1971, als die 750er Laverda-Langstreckenrennmaschine eine Durchschnittsgeschwindigkeit von 125,26 km/h erreichte und das 24-Stunden-Rennen von Oss in Holland gewann. Auf gut deutsch: Der kernige Twin fuhr die etablierten Marken Triumph, Honda, Suzuki, Kawasaki, Moto Guzzi und Ducati in Grund und Boden. Die Rennmaschine basierte auf der 750er-Straßenversion, wurde allerdings fachmännisch getunt. Nach der Kur brachte der Parallel-Twin 70 PS und beschleunigte den Racer auf über 220 km/h. Was für die Piste taugt, wäre auch auf den öffentlichen Straßen gut, sagten sich die Laverda-Bosse. Ab 1972 gab es diese Rennmaschine genau so für die Straße mit der Modellbezeichnung 750 SFC zu kaufen.

He is to motorcycle racing what British World Champion racecar driver Lewis Hamilton is to Formula One racing. Indeed, one might say he all but steals the limelight from most other heroes on this incomplete heroes' list. He's the kind of dude who develops goose bumps remembering the old days when "one out of two or three races ended in a fatality." Giacomo Agostini is considered one of the best motorcycle racing pros of all time. You can't even see a complete list of all his victories on the Internet without scrolling down. We're talking 15 World Championship titles, 14 Italian Championship titles—including one in Italian hill climb events, 6 Isle of Man TT victories (taken at average speeds of 104 mph with no sweat), one victory at the Daytona 200, and another one at the 200 Miles of Imola ... there are just too many to list them all. To make a long story short, Giacomo Agostini can boast 122 Grand Prix victories in 186 races—virtually all of them on MV Agusta. In 1977, Barry Sheene nabbed the 500 cc World Championship title from him—and "Ago" subsequently retired from his active career. He still likes to crack the throttle, though, back home in the city of Bergamo in Lombardy, riding his old MV Agusta 500. Of course, what else?

Er ist der Lewis Hamilton auf zwei Rädern. Der, neben dem so ziemlich alle auf dieser unvollständigen Helden-liste ein bisschen alt aussehen. Der, der Gänsehaut be-kommt, wenn er an früher denkt, denn „da starb alle zwei, drei Rennen ein Pilot". Giacomo Agostini gilt als einer der besten Motorradrennfahrer aller Zeiten. Und wer im Internet seine Siegesbilanz ansehen möchte, der kommt nicht umhin, nach unten zu scrollen. Denn es passt nicht alles auf einen Bildschirm. Da wären 15 Weltmeistertitel, 14 italienische Meistertitel – darunter einer als italienischer Bergmeister, 6 Isle-of-Man-TT-Siege mit Durchschnittsgeschwindigkeiten von gerne mal 167 km/h, ein Sieg bei der Daytona 200 und den 200 Mei-len von Imola ... das würde hier den Rahmen sprengen. Kurz: 122 Grand-Prix-Siege bei 186 Rennen. Nahezu alle auf MV Agusta. Barry Sheene luchste ihm 1977 den Titel in der 500-cm³-Klasse ab – „Ago" beendet daraufhin sei-ne aktive Karriere. Und gibt auch heute noch gerne Gas. Zu Hause in Bergamo. Auf seiner alten MV Agusta 500. Was sonst!

GIACOMO AGOSTINI

 # TONI MANG

Actually, his full name is Anton Mang. He's a toolmaker by trade and former ski bob champion of Germany. He once played the part of the rooster in the film adaptation of the German folktale *The Town Musicians of Bremen*— but that's not what this is about. "Toni" is the moniker he chose for himself, and that's how he went down in motorcycling history. Oh yeah, he's also a five-time motorcycle racing champion. All right, let's go back to the beginning, he was 18 years old when he first took part in a motorcycle road racing event. Hang on, are you ready for this? He followed up on it by winning the German Championship in 1975, riding a 350-cc Yamaha. One year later, he won his first World Championship race, the Grand Prix of Germany at the Nürburgring. After that, Kawasaki signed him up as factory rider, and it's safe to say he had a superb run. In 1981, Toni Mang became Double World Champion—to be chosen Athlete of the Year shortly thereafter. He then went on to defend his 350 cc World Championship title on Kawasaki, earning the distinction "Everlasting World Champion" before moving up to the 500-cc class. Today this native of Bavaria can proudly look back on 154 starts in the Motorcycle World Championship, 84 podium places, 42 victories, 34 pole positions, and 26 of the fastest laps measured.

Eigentlich heißt er Anton Mang, ist gelernter Werkzeugmacher, deutscher Skibobmeister und besetzte einst die Hauptrolle im Film über die „Bremer Stadtmusikanten" – aber darum geht es jetzt gar nicht. Toni will er heißen, und als solcher ging er auch in die Motorradgeschichte ein. Als fünffacher Motorradweltmeister. Aber eins nach dem anderen. Mit 18 Jahren nahm Toni an seinem ersten Motorradstraßenrennen teil. Festhalten, jetzt geht's los: Es folgte der deutsche Meisterschaftsgewinn im Jahr 1975 auf einer 350-cm^3-Yamaha. Ein Jahr später gewann er sein erstes WM-Rennen, den Grand Prix von Deutschland auf dem Nürburgring. Kawasaki engagierte ihn als Werksfahrer; man kann sagen, Mang hatte einen super Lauf. 1981 wurde Mang Doppelweltmeister – kurz danach zum Sportler des Jahres gewählt. Er verteidigte seinen WM-Titel in der 350-cm^3-Klasse auf Kawasaki und verdiente sich das Attribut „ewiger Weltmeister", bevor er in die Königsklasse wechselte: 500 cm^3. Heute blickt der Bayer zurück auf 154 Starts in der Motorrad-WM, auf 84 Podiumsplätze, 42 Siege, 34 Polepositions und 26 schnellste Rennrunden.

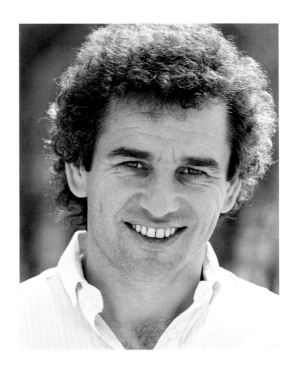

TECH SPECS

ENGINE:

V2, four-stroke

POWER:

53 kW (71 hp) at 6,700 rpm

DISPLACEMENT:

844 cc

PRODUCTION:

1975–1980

It was a time when being athletic was just becoming hip, especially in northern Italy, where the two major players were the Ducati 750 SS and the Laverda 750 SFC. In order to keep up, Moto Guzzi needed a major player of its own. At the Milan Motorcycle Show in 1975, the company presented its latest ride, the Le Mans 1. Looking equally aggressive and handsome, this bike featured a four-stroke V2 with 71 hp, an increased compression ratio of 10:1, a bigger cam, a pair of 1.5-inch Dell'Orto pumper carbs, handlebar stubs and semi-cowling. This Italian player with its Guzzi-typical shaft drive had no problem delivering top speeds north of 125 mph. The 850 Le Mans 1 remains one of the most sought after V2 Guzzis among collectors to this very day.

Sportlichkeit war gerade hip, besonders in der norditalienischen Nachbarschaft. Profiathleten waren die Ducati 750 SS und die Laverda 750 SFC. Dem musste Moto Guzzi etwas entgegenhalten. Auf der Mailänder Motorradmesse präsentierte das Werk 1975 die Le Mans 1. Aggressiv und schön zugleich: mit dickem V2-Viertaktmotor, 71 PS, auf 10:1 erhöhte Verdichtung, scharfer Nockenwelle, zwei 36er-Dell'Orto-Vergasern, Stummellenker und Halbverkleidung. Der italienische Sportler mit Guzzi-typischem Kardanantrieb brachte es auf mehr als 200 km/h. Noch heute zählt die 850 Le Mans 1 unter Sammlern zu den begehrtesten V2-Guzzis überhaupt.

MOTO GUZZI
850 Le Mans 1

In the 1950s, Moto Guzzi's two-cylinder V2 failed to catch on with anyone except the Italian military, which decided to plant the engine in one of its vehicles. Still, the company continued to make good money building robust motorbikes with up to 500 cc at the time. In the mid-1960s, however, Europe's motorcycle industry slid into a severe crisis, and Moto Guzzi suddenly struggled to stay afloat as well. The company needed a big bike, and they needed it soon. Incidentally, a powerful V2 engine was already in the works and, in 1967, the company pulled off a miracle: The Moto Guzzi V7 quickly conquered the hearts of touring enthusiasts and sidecar owners. The 700-cc power plant of the V7 was virtually indestructible, its shaft drive required very little maintenance while its handling characteristics and ride comfort were second to none. With their new 50-hp V7, Moto Guzzi indeed had a top seller. It laid the foundation for a whole range of triumphant motorbikes that were to follow from Moto Guzzi.

So wirklich interessierte sich in den Fünfzigerjahren niemand für das V2-Einbauaggregat von Moto Guzzi. Außer den Behörden, die den Motor in ein Militärfahrzeug einpflanzen ließen. Mit der Herstellung von robusten Motorrädern bis 500 Kubik verdiente das Werk damals gutes Geld. Mitte der Sechzigerjahre rutschte die europäische Motorradbranche in eine schwere Krise, auch Moto Guzzi kämpfte ums Überleben. Jetzt musste ein großes Motorrad her, ein dicker V2-Motor stand bereits auf der Werkbank. 1967 war das Wunder vollbracht, die Moto Guzzi V7 fuhr sich in die Herzen der Tourenfahrer und Gespanntreiber. Das 700er-Triebwerk war unverwüstlich, der Kardanantrieb wartungsarm, Fahrverhalten und Fahrkomfort erste Klasse. Mit der neuen, 50 PS starken V7 gelang Moto Guzzi ein Topseller. Der Urahn aller bis heute gebauten Guzzis war geboren.

TECH SPECS

ENGINE:

V2, four-stroke

POWER:

37 kW (50 hp) at 6,500 rpm

DISPLACEMENT:

757 cc

PRODUCTION:

1969–1976

MOTO GUZZI
V7 Special

Four criteria are essential for a dual-sport motorcycle: Ergonomics, luggage, steering behavior, and range. In all of these points, the Stelvio has the highest ratings for some time. This 617-pound machine also effortlessly corners tight curves. The 105-hp air-cooled two-cylinder engine nicely obliges here and, after 4,500 rpm, faithfully races onward, conditions permitting.

Für eine Reiseenduro gibt es vier ausschlaggebende Kriterien: Ergonomie, Gepäck, Lenkverhalten und Reichweite. In all diesen Punkten schneidet die Stelvio schon seit geraumer Zeit mit Bestbewertungen ab. Die 280 kg Gewicht lassen sich auch durch enge Ecken handlich dirigieren, der luftgekühlte Zweizylinder mit 105 PS arbeitet dabei äußerst zuvorkommend und packt ab 4500 Umdrehungen dann auch mal ehrlich zu, wenn es denn sein darf.

TECH SPECS

ENGINE:

V2

POWER:

77 kW (105 hp) at 7,250 rpm

DISPLACEMENT:

1,151 cc

MOTO GUZZI
Stelvio 1200 8V NTX

TECH SPECS

ENGINE:

V2

POWER:

77 kW (105 hp)

DISPLACEMENT:

1,151 cc

MOTO GUZZI
Norge 1200 GT 8V

A tubular steel double-cradle frame and a rock solid 1,151-cc twin engine with a cardan shaft running to the rear wheel in a single-sided swing arm: That's the basis for Moto Guzzi to build the 1200 Sport, Griso, Stelvio, and Norge models. Logically, the tried and tested body also makes perfect sense for the Norge sports tourer, highlighting its touring capability with a comfortable seating position. What's more, due to a more flexible chassis, this version takes tight corners with the usual Guzzi finesse.

Ein Doppelschleifen-Stahlrohrrahmen und ein grundsolider 1151-cm³-Zweizylinder mit einer in eine Einarmschwinge verlaufenden Kardanwelle zum Hinterrad. Das ist die Grundlage, und auf dieser baut Moto Guzzi sowohl die 1200 Sport, Griso, Stelvio und Norge auf. Logisch, dass der bewährte Aufbau auch für den Sporttourer Norge Sinn macht und nicht nur seine Reisetauglichkeit bei komfortabler Sitzposition unterstreicht, sondern darüber hinaus dank wendigem Chassis auch enge Kurven in gewohnter Guzzi-Manier nimmt.

TECH SPECS

ENGINE:

V2

POWER:

71 kW (97 hp) at 6,500 rpm

DISPLACEMENT:

1,380 CC

MOTO GUZZI
California 1400 Touring

It's a genuine offer: Anyone who wants to do without an automobile would be happy to have the 1400 to fall back on, so claims the manufacturer. Thanks to the panniers, windshield, and the amount of space provided, this is not so far out, at least for couples without any children, especially if the weather is good. If not, the engine settings range from "wet" through "touring" to "fast." Thanks to the low seat and corresponding low center of gravity, the comfort level is admirably high, even at walking pace.

Das Angebot ist selbstbewusst formuliert: Wer auf das Auto verzichten mag, der könne gerne auf die 1400 Touring zurückgreifen, so der Hersteller. Dank Koffern, Windschild und Platzangebot ist dieses Angebot zumindest für kinderlose Paare gar nicht so weit hergeholt, zumal dann nicht, wenn das Wetter mitspielt. Falls nicht, reichen die Einstellungen für den Motor von „Regen" über „touristisch" bis „zügig". Dank niedriger Sitzposition und einem ebensolchen Schwerpunkt ist der Fahrkomfort schon ab Schrittgeschwindigkeit auf hohem Niveau.

Technically, the changes compared to the V7 Special are obvious: Fully adjustable twin turbo MacPherson struts with a header tank on the rear axle. Visually, however, the Racer packs 90 years of MG history into a 50-hp recreational bike: A single-seater with a 5-gallon chrome-plated metal tank, perforated brushed aluminum side and carburetor covers, a red tubular double-cradle frame, and lots of chrome and polished metal.

Technisch sind die Änderungen gegenüber der V7 Special überschaubar: voll einstellbare Biturbo-Federbeine mit Ausgleichsbehälter an der Hinterachse. Optisch dagegen packt die Racer 90 Jahre MG-Geschichte in ein 50-PS-Genuss-Bike: Ein Einsitzer mit verchromten 22-Liter-Metalltank, Seitendeckeln und Vergaserabdeckungen aus gebürstetem und gelochtem Aluminium, einem rot lackierter Doppelschleifen-Rohrrahmen und jede Menge Chrom und blankem Metall.

TECH SPECS

ENGINE:

V2

POWER:

37 kW (50 hp) at 6,800 rpm

DISPLACEMENT:

744 CC

MOTO GUZZI
V7 750 Racer

It took Alfonso Morini a couple of years to make his international breakthrough. Not as a racing rider, but as founder of his own motorcycle company. In 1973, the company's top of the line model was its exquisite 3½-liter bike. Back in the day, this high-performance motorbike was one of the easiest to handle in the 350-cc class. Its power plant was a simple and low-maintenance four-stroke OHV V2 with Heron flat-face cylinder heads, surprisingly low fuel consumption and remarkable workmanship. The V2 was designed by constructor legend Franco Lambertini and gave this 34-hp cult bike a top speed of almost 95 mph.

Es hat ein paar Jährchen gedauert, bis Alfonso Morini seinen internationalen Durchbruch hatte. Nicht als Rennfahrer, sondern mit der eigenen Motorradfirma Moto Morini. Zum Spitzenmodell wurde 1973 die filigrane 3 ½. In der 350er-Klasse damals eine der handlichsten Sportmaschinen. Herzstück war ein simpler und wartungsfreundlicher sowie im Benzinverbrauch günstiger OHV-V2-Viertakt-Motor, mit Heron-Brennräumen in den Zylinderköpfen und unglaublich guter Verarbeitung. Entwickelt hatte das Triebwerk der legendäre Motorradkonstrukteur Franco Lambertini. Der 34 PS starke Sportler schaffte auch ohne Rückenwind fast 160 Sachen.

TECH SPECS

ENGINE:

V2, four-stroke

POWER:

25 kW (34 hp) at 6,850 rpm

DISPLACEMENT:

344 cc

MOTO MORINI

3 1/2

PRODUCTION:

1973–1983

TECH SPECS

ENGINE:

Four-cylinder in-line, four-stroke

POWER:

65 kW (88 hp) at 6,500 rpm

DISPLACEMENT:

1,197 CC

PRODUCTION:

1968–1980

Friedel Münch was by any means an engineering genius. A race driver and engine tuner, he used to work as a race mechanic for German motorcycle maker Horex before managing his own workshop. By 1966, he used his small business to build the world's first super bike. A super bike ahead of its time, it was equipped with a 1,000-cc four-cylinder car engine borrowed from NSU, delivering 55 hp and capable of speeds north of 110 mph. Mighty as a mammoth, this bike was—hence its name. The only problem was that this was a trademark-protected logo, so Münch changed the name of his bike creations to Münch-4. In 1968, he followed up on the original 55-hp 1,000-cc and 1,100-cc versions with the legendary Münch-4 TTS 1200, which developed 88 hp and topped out at over 125 mph. By the time the company was liquidated in 1980, a total of 478 Münch-4 bikes had been built.

Friedel Münch war ein genialer Tüftler. Erst Rennfahrer und Schrauber in Personalunion, zwischendurch Rennmechaniker bei Horex und dann Kfz-Meister in seiner eigenen Werkstatt. 1966 stellte der Hesse als Konstrukteur, Erfinder und Hersteller in seiner kleinen Firma das weltweit erste Big Bike auf die Räder. Eine Maschine, die ihrer Zeit voraus war, mit 1000er-Vierzylinder-NSU-Automotor, 55 PS kräftig und 180 Sachen schnell. Mächtig wie ein Mammut, daher der Name. Das Logo war allerdings geschützt, und so nannte Münch fortan seine Werke Münch-4. Nach den ersten Ausführungen mit 1000 und 1100 cm³ und 55 PS folgte 1968 die zur Legende gewordene Münch-4 TTS 1200 mit 88 PS und über 200 km/h Spitze. Bis zur Firmenschließung 1980 entstanden 478 Münch-4-Motorräder.

MÜNCH
4 TTS 1200 Mammut

TECH SPECS

ENGINE:

Four-cylinder in-line, four-stroke

POWER:

55 kW (75 hp) at 8,500 rpm

DISPLACEMENT:

789 cc

PRODUCTION:

1975–1977

MV AGUSTA
750 Sport America

Most motorcycle enthusiasts have at least a fleeting knowledge of the early-1970s MV Agusta 750 S. Barely four years after launching the 750 S for production, MV Agusta found itself in financial peril and came under government control in 1974. Desperate for cash, the company focused product development on driving up its market share in the US. Indeed, the days of classic round shapes and the big old drum brake on the front wheel were over. With capacity increased to nearly 800 cc and horsepower boosted to 75 hp, MV's new super bike topped out at more than 130 mph. The design of the cowling followed the zeitgeist of the 1970s: Modern dual disc brakes on the front wheel, a sturdy gas tank, angular seat, and black-coated tailpipes.

In der Motorradszene kennt fast jeder die legendäre MV Agusta 750S aus den frühen Siebzigerjahren. Nicht einmal vier Jahre nach Produktionsbeginn geriet das italienische Unternehmen in finanzielle Notlage. Im Jahr 1974 kam es unter staatliche Verwaltung, Geld musste reinkommen, ein absatzstarkes Bike für den US-amerikanischen Markt entwickelt werden. Die klassischen Rundungen und die große Trommelbremse im Vorderrad gehörten der Vergangenheit an. Den Hubraum vergrößerte man auf knapp 800 Kubik, die Leistung auf 75 PS, Topspeed erreichte der neue Supersportler über 210 km/h. Beim Outfit trug man dem Zeitgeist Rechnung: moderne Doppelscheibenbremse am Vorderrad, bulliger Tank, kantige Sitzbank, schwarz lackierte Schalldämpfer.

If your garage houses a well-preserved MV Agusta 750 S these days, you've got a precious gem right there. Did you know that only 583 of these fairly exclusive rides were ever built following their debut in 1970? The 750 S succeeded the 600 model, which had basically flopped due its overweight lackluster appearance, like it had all the touring but no game. The 750 S, on the other hand, was a bona fide super bike with 72 hp and capable of up to 125 mph, thanks to a capacity boost up to 750 cc. It sported four tailpipes best described as technological works of art. Rounding off its dynamic appearance and driving experience, MV constructors gave the 750 S handlebar stubs, streamlined gas tank, sports seating, and rear-mounted footrests. Think racing flair in its purest imaginable form.

Wer eine gut gepflegte MV Agusta 750 S in der Garage stehen hat, der hütet dort einen kostbaren Schatz. Denn das ab 1970 verkaufte Bike ist höchst exklusiv – genauer gesagt wurden nur 583 Exemplare gebaut. Vorgänger der legendären 750 S war das Modell 600, das mangels Formschönheit eher floppte. Zu unsportlich, zu dröge – Tourenmaschine eben. Die gut 200 km/h schnelle und 72 PS starke Sportmaschine wiederum erhielt eine Hubraumerweiterung auf 750 cm³, die vier Auspuffrohre kamen einem technischen Kunstwerk gleich. Für die sportliche Optik und das Fahrgefühl spendierten die MV-Konstrukteure der 750 S Stummellenker, Sporttank, Sportsitzbank und hinten liegende Fußrasten. Mehr reinrassiges Racingflair war kaum machbar.

TECH SPECS

ENGINE:

Four-cylinder in-line, four-stroke

POWER:

53 kW (72 hp) at 9,200 rpm

DISPLACEMENT:

743 cc

PRODUCTION:

1970–1975

MV AGUSTA
750 S

Think Norton Motorcycles and the legendary and infamous Isle of Man Tourist Trophy race will spring to mind! No other manufacturer has claimed victory there so often. There can be no doubt that a machine with the Norton badge must have certain features. The Commando 961 SF is a case in point. Because where other café racers get by with a pint-size capacity, with almost double the volume and 80 hp, the Norton makes a clear statement. Radial Brembo brakes then slow everything down again.

Wer an Norton Motorcycles denkt, denkt automatisch auch an die legendäre und berüchtigte Tourist Trophy auf der Isle of Man. Kein anderer Hersteller gewann dort häufiger. Es steht also außer Zweifel, dass eine Maschine mit dem Norton-Emblem gewisse Merkmale aufweisen muss. Die Commando 961 SF ist hierfür das beste Beispiel. Denn wo andere Café Racer mit einem halben Liter Hubraum auskommen, setzt die Norton mit fast dem doppelten Volumen und 80 PS ein deutliches Statement. Radiale Brembo-Stopper fangen dann alles wieder ein.

TECH SPECS

ENGINE:

Parallel twin

POWER:

59 kW (80 hp) at 6,500 rpm

DISPLACEMENT:

961 cc

NORTON
Commando 961 SF

TECH SPECS

ENGINE:

Four-cylinder, two-stroke

POWER:

70 kW (95 hp) at 9,500 rpm

DISPLACEMENT:

498 cc

PRODUCTION:

1984–1987

SUZUKI
RG 500 GAMMA

Launching a superbike is usually done in one of two ways: Take a street bike that's fast and furious and turn it into a race bike or take a race bike and turn it into a street bike that's even more fast and furious. With its RG 500 Gamma, Suzuki came up with a third way: Take whatever's left. Sorry if this seems like a disparaging way to put it, but after legends like Barry Sheene or Lucky Marco Lucchinelli enjoyed victory after victory on this machine back in the mid-1970s, it became the racing equivalent of a lame duck by the early 1980s. Alright, said the engineers at Suzuki, let's put it on the street! The only problem was when they decided for the Grand Prix powerhouse of the RG 500 to share the same gearbox with the RG 400, which was shy of almost 40 hp. The number of resulting engine failures was itself legendary. New features included two tailpipes in the rear cowl.

Ein Superbike findet im Allgemeinen auf zwei Wegen zum Marktplatz: Entweder es geht als Straßenbike ab wie Luzi und man baut es dann zum Renner um, oder man nutzt die Erkenntnisse aus der Rennserie, um einen fulminanten Streetfighter zu kreieren. Suzuki fand bei der RG 500 Gamma einen dritten Weg: die Resteverwertung. Etwas despektierlich, Verzeihung, aber nachdem Mitte der Siebzigerjahre Legenden wie Barry Sheene oder Lucky Marco Lucchinelli mit der Maschine Erfolge gefeiert hatten, geriet sie Anfang der Achtzigerjahre zum *lame duck*. Macht nix, sagten sich die Iwataer, dann stellen wir sie halt auf die Straße. Allerdings gönnten sie dem Grand-Prix-Triebwerk anfänglich nur das Getriebe der knapp 40 PS schwächeren RG 400, was einige legendäre Motorbrüche zeitigte. Neu waren die zwei Auspuffe im Heckbürzel.

KEVIN SCHWANTZ

His racing style? Legendary. His mouth? Plenty big. His racing number? The one and only. Schwantz wrote history as one of the most popular motorcycle road racers ever. His unforgettable quotes include the one about braking before turns, "Get hard braking done early; don't wait till you see God!" The native Texan with the racing number 34 certainly stirred up the 500 cc Superbike National Championships from 1986 to 1995. In 1993, he won and was World Champion; having finished second, third, and fourth place the previous three years. Upon his retirement from motorcycle racing, the FIM paid him respect by retiring his racing number (34). Loathe to resting upon his laurels, Schwantz now spends his days owning and operating a motorcycle riding school out of his home in Texas.

Sein Fahrstil? Legendär. Sein Mundwerk? Gewagt. Seine Startnummer? Unvergeben. Kevin Schwantz hat als einer der beliebtesten Rennfahrer Geschichte geschrieben. Unvergessen ist unter anderem sein Spruch über das Anbremsen vor Kurven: „Wenn du Gott siehst, dann musst du bremsen". Der Texaner mit der Startnummer 34 mischte die 500-cm³-Klasse der Motorrad-WM von 1986 bis 1995 ordentlich auf. Im Jahr 1993 wurde er Weltmeister, die drei Jahre zuvor belegte er die Plätze zwei, drei und vier. Zu seinen Ehren wird seine Startnummer 34 nicht mehr in der Königsklasse der Motorradweltmeisterschaft vergeben. Und weil der 50-Jährige keine Lust hat, sich auf seinen Lorbeeren auszuruhen, macht er es auch nicht. Sondern betreibt eine Motorradrennfahrerschule in seiner Heimat Texas.

They were both fast and loose, the 1970s as much as Barry Sheene. Indeed, his track record as double 500 cc World Champion isn't the only reason why this British motorcycle road racer remains unforgotten among motor racing fans. He has also been credited with opening the door for rock 'n' roll to find its way into motor racing. Barry Sheene loved parties, women, and publicity. He once refused to race in the Isle of Man TT, because he "didn't see any point in beating the clock by racing alone in a constant downpour." He went on to say that the event was neither his race, nor was it his idea of a race, and that the event proved once and for all that everything came down to "how well you know the course." Hardly any less dangerous than the Isle of Man TT, however, was one of his oldest hobbies, which ultimately may have cost him his life in 2003: Sheene had been smoking ever since he was a kid. In fact, he was such a hardcore chain smoker he even drilled a hole into the chin section of his helmet, just so he could keep puffing away. But let's remember him as a successful racing pro and businessman instead. Because that's exactly what he was, dangerous hobbies notwithstanding.

Schnell und freizügig waren sie beide. Die Siebzigerjahre ebenso wie Barry Sheene. Der britische Motorrad-rennfahrer bleibt allerdings nicht nur als zweifacher 500er-Weltmeister unvergessen in der Szene. Sondern auch, weil er derjenige war, der den Rock 'n' Roll in den Rennsport brachte. Sheene liebte Partys, Frauen und die Aufmerksamkeit. Verweigerte seine Teilnahme bei der Isle of Man TT, weil er „keinen Sinne darin sieht, alleine gegen die Uhr im strömenden Regen herumzufahren". Schließlich sei das nicht sein Verständnis von Rennen und beweise allemal, „wie gut du die Strecke kennst". Ähnlich gefährlich wie die Isle of Man TT war auch eines seiner frühesten Hobbys, das ihm möglicherweise im Jahr 2003 das Leben kostete: Sheene hat bereits als Kind geraucht. Später war er ein so durchgeknallter Ketten-raucher, dass er sich sogar ein Loch ins Kinnteil des Helms bohrte, um jederzeit an seinen Kippen ziehen zu können. Behalten wir ihn lieber als erfolgreichen Renn-fahrer und Geschäftsmann in Erinnerung. Denn genau das war er. Gefährliche Hobbys hin oder her.

 # BARRY SHEENE

In the early 1980s, Suzuki slid into a deep crisis. The only way out of it was by direct intervention from corporate headquarters. As part of corporate strategy beginning in October 1984, Suzuki sent some of its managers along with a small number of dedicated staff members from Japan to Germany to assume operations at its new subsidiary "Suzuki Motor GmbH Deutschland" in the town of Heppenheim. It was around this time that Suzuki presented its next milestone, the GSX-R 750. Here was an aluminum-framed race bike equally at home on public roads—right away, everybody began referring to it as the new superbike. By launching this sizzling hot ride, Suzuki became the new standard setter in the design of street performance bikes. When does the GSX-R 750 max out? Not until you hit 173 mph.

Anfang der Achtzigerjahre rutschte Suzuki in eine tiefe Krise. Als Ausweg blieb nur der Eingriff vom Stammwerk. Ab Oktober 1984 kam das Management direkt aus Japan und brachte mit einem kleinen Stab engagierter Mitarbeiter die neu gegründete „Suzuki Motor GmbH Deutschland" wieder nach Heppenheim. Zeitgleich präsentierte sie den nächsten Überknaller: die GSX-R 750. Ein Rennmotorrad mit Alu-Rahmen für die öffentliche Straße – und plötzlich sprach alle Welt nur noch vom Superbike. Mit dieser Heizerkiste war Suzuki von nun an im Bau von sportlichen Straßenmotorrädern das Maß der Dinge. Schluss mit dem Vortrieb? Erst bei 278 km/h.

TECH SPECS

ENGINE:

Four-cylinder, four-stroke

POWER:

110 kW (150 hp) at 13,200 rpm

DISPLACEMENT:

750 cc

SUZUKI
GSX-R 750

TECH SPECS

SUZUKI
GSX-S 1000

ENGINE:

In-line, four-stroke

POWER:

107 kW (145 hp) at 9,500 rpm

DISPLACEMENT:

999 CC

Care to delve into the history of Suzuki? Then, you're highly likely to get to the roots of the GSX-R in 1976 and to discover the GS 750. You'll be aware that this was not only Suzuki's first in-line four-cylinder four-stroke engine, but also a naked bike. And the GSX-S 1000 follows in exactly the same tradition. Over the years, the 16-valve water-cooled engine has been consistently developed and now boasts a 999-cc displacement.

Wer in der Geschichte von Suzuki kramt, wird im Jahr 1976 auf die Wurzeln der GSX-R stoßen und die GS 750 entdecken. Und er wird feststellen: Sie war nicht nur Suzukis erster Viertakt-Reihenvierzylinder, sondern auch ein Naked Bike. Und genau an diese Tradition schließt die GSX-S 1000 an. Über die Jahre wurde der wassergekühlte Motor mit 16 Ventilen konsequent weiterentwickelt und kommt heute auf 999 cm3.

If the GSX-S 1000 comes across as too light, with the "F," for "facing," you can order a few more elements. Technically, the sister machines are practically identical. The 999-cc four-cylinder has been optimized and works with 16 valves, water-cooling, and electronic engine control. In addition to the all-round full facing below, the front windshield should be of interest to touring bikers.

Wem die GSX-S 1000 irgendwie zu luftig daherkommt, der kann sich mit dem „F" wie „Facing" (Verkleidung) noch etwas drumherum dazubestellen. Technisch sind die beiden Schwestern nahezu identisch. Der 999-cm³-Vierzylinder wurde optimiert, arbeitet mit 16 Ventilen, Wasserkühlung und elektronischer Motorsteuerung. Neben der Vollverkleidung unterrum dürfte bei Tourenfahrern vor allem das Windschild vorn Interesse wecken.

TECH SPECS

ENGINE:

Four-cylinder in-line

POWER:

107 kW (145 hp) at 9,500 rpm

DISPLACEMENT:

999 CC

SUZUKI
GSX-S 1000 F

TECH SPECS

ENGINE:

Two-cylinder, four-stroke

POWER:

27 kW (37 hp) at 6,500 rpm

DISPLACEMENT:

499 CC

PRODUCTION:

1959–1974

TRIUMPH
T 100 C 500 Trophy

All of their superbikes were proving a major success for Triumph, and sales figures for their small motorbikes were impressive too. What the company lacked in its lineup was something in the middle. To fill the gap, Triumph launched the 500 Trophy. Light, easy to handle, but also fast and tough, this bike offered motorcycle fun on the go. It further served as a basis for subsequent enduro versions that would prove their tenacity and endurance in many enduro races, including various six-day races. It's not by accident that enduro is an acronym for endurance and *duro*, which is Spanish for "hard."

Triumph feierte gerade tolle Erfolge mit seinen Superbikes, und auch die kleinen Krafträder verkauften sich recht ordentlich. Was fehlte, war der Mittler zwischen den Welten, und so schufen sie die 500 Trophy, ein handliches, leichtes, aber auch schnelles und zähes Bike für den Motorradhunger zwischendurch. Sie diente auch als Basis für die Enduro-Versionen, die ihren Biss und Durchhaltevermögen bei vielen Enduro-Wettbewerben, darunter verschiedene Sechs-Tage-Rennen, beweisen konnten. Enduro ist eine Wortkreation aus dem spanischen *duro* = hart und dem englischen *endurance* = Ausdauer.

TECH SPECS

ENGINE:

Parallel twin

POWER:

50 kW (68 hp) at 7,500 rpm

DISPLACEMENT:

865 cc

TRIUMPH
Bonneville T100 Black

Don't get me wrong, as no one should ever gain the impression that the standard Bonneville is a tame entry-level bike, but with the T100 Black, it has found its mean and much more striking sister: Exactly in the style of a custom bike, it has black, spoked wheels, milled radiator fins, a black engine housing, black handlebars, and mirrors at the front. At its heart, as ever, is the 68-hp 865-cc twin engine.

Bitte nicht falsch verstehen, es soll hier keinesfalls der Eindruck entstehen, die serienmäßige Bonneville sei ein zahmes Einsteiger-Bike, aber mit der T100 Black findet sie eben ihre böse und deutlich markantere Schwester: Ganz im Stile eines Custom Bikes rollt sie mit schwarzen Felgen, Speichenrädern, gefrästen Kühlrippen und schwarzem Motorgehäuse sowie schwarzen Lenkern und Spiegeln vor. Im Kern arbeitet dabei nach wie vor der 865-cm³-Zweizylinder mit 68 PS.

This bike would go on to become the absolute hit. Working with an engine producing 42 hp, engineers at Triumph intended to reach a speed of 120 mph. So, in 1956, they went to test their new engine at Bonneville Salt Flats in Utah. Riding the streamlined fully clad machine, test driver Johnny Allen didn't brake until he hit an absolutely stunning 214 mph. The Britons took the engine along with the name and went on in 1959 to not only create one of the most awesome and fastest motorcycles, but also one of the biggest winners in the motorcycle racing series. The 1968 model has been called the "best Bonnie there ever was."

Dieses Motorrad sollte der absolute Kracher werden. Triumph wollte mit knapp 42 PS auf eine Geschwindigkeit von 120 mph, also über 190 km/h kommen und testete den neuen Motor 1956 auf dem Bonneville-Salzsee in Utah. Auf der stromlinienförmig vollverkleideten Maschine bremste Testfahrer Johnny Allen erst bei 345 km/h. Die Briten übernahmen Motor und Namen und kreierten ab 1959 nicht nur eines der schönsten und schnellsten, sondern auch erfolgreichsten Motorräder bei Serienmaschinenrennen. Die Version von 1968 gilt als die beste Bonnie, die es je gab.

TECH SPECS

ENGINE:

Two-cylinder, four-stroke

POWER:

35 kW (47 hp) at 6,700 rpm

DISPLACEMENT:

649 cc

PRODUCTION:

1959–1973

TRIUMPH
T120 Bonneville 650

TECH SPECS

ENGINE:

Three-cylinder in-line

POWER:

99 kW (135 hp) at 9,400 rpm

DISPLACEMENT:

1,050 cc

TRIUMPH

Speed Triple ABS

If the challenge is a winding track prepared with smoothed asphalt through the south of France, then the Speed Triple ABS is the perfect answer. Signature features of the Triumph are three cylinders and 135 hp, and this bike has no superfluous gimmicks. In the spirit of the naked bike, this is a pure riding machine and awesome accelerator. The radial Brembo 4-piston brake calipers on the front wheel work together with an ABS system that makes 100 calculations per second to prevent the front wheel from locking.

Wenn die Herausforderung in einer kurvenreichen mit flachgebügeltem Asphalt präparierten Piste durch Südfrankreich besteht, ist die Speed Triple ABS die perfekte Antwort. Triumph-typisch mit Dreizylinder und 135 PS, verzichtet das Bike auf jeglichen, überflüssigen Schnickschnack, sondern versteht sich ganz im Sinne der Naked Bikes als pure Fahrmaschine und Wirkbeschleuniger. Die radial montierten Brembo-4-Kolben-Bremssättel am Vorderrad arbeiten zusammen mit einem ABS, das pro Sekunde 100 Berechnungen durchführt, um ein Blockieren des Vorderrads zu verhindern.

The race is on: New radiator fins, shock absorbers with a fuller sound, and chrome chain guard. Plus a color-matched handlebar cover with a stripe detail, which is now a standard feature as is the seat cowl. New elements, and then some. Familiar features include the short handlebars and sculpted seat, back-set footrests, alloy wheels, and adjustable rear wheel suspension for a more sporty riding experience.

The Race is on: Neue Kühlrippen, Schalldämpfer mit satterem Sound und verchromter Kettenschutz. Dazu kommt eine Lenkerverkleidung in Fahrzeugfarbe mit Zierstreifen, die jetzt ebenso wie die Höckerabdeckung serienmäßig ist. Das ist neu. Etabliert sind dagegen die Stummellenker und Sitzbankhöcker, nach hinten versetzte Fußrasten, Leichtmetallfelgen und die einstellbare Hinterradfederung für das sportliche Fahrgefühl.

TECH SPECS

ENGINE:

Parallel twin

POWER:

50 kW (69 hp) at 7,400 rpm

DISPLACEMENT:

865 cc

TRIUMPH

Thruxton

In the early 1970s, many urban cowboys setting out to be "real bikers" naturally had to have big, heavy bikes to proudly call their own—like the 750-cc Hondas and Kawasaki 900 Z1s. At the same time, in order to boost the sales pitch for their smaller motorcycles, Yamaha equipped both the RD 250 and its larger sibling, the RD 350, with two-stroke engines primarily designed for high speed. In no time at all, the nickname "crotch rockets" was born. The real problem, however, was the extra space necessary to carry their own special tool kits. Blame it on the combination of high rpm's and air-cooling that left their engines prone to failures. Meanwhile, the hobby mechanics out there had to devote all their passion to fixing them.

Anfang der Siebzigerjahre fuhr der wahre Biker die großen Wuchtbrummen: die 750er-Honda oder die 900 Z1 von Kawasaki. Um auch kleinen Hubräumern Argumente für einen Verkauf an die Hand zu geben, richtete Yamaha die RD 250 und ihre große Schwester RD 350, beides Zweitakter, vor allem auf Geschwindigkeit aus. Ruckzuck war der Spitzname geboren: Taschenraketen. Allerdings musste die Tasche anfangs groß genug sein, um auch noch einen Raketenwerkzeugkoffer zu beherbergen – die hohen Drehzahlen und die Luftkühlung machten die Motoren sehr anfällig und sorgten regelmäßig dafür, dass der passionierte Schrauber auch ausgiebig seiner Leidenschaft frönen konnte.

TECH SPECS

ENGINE:

Two-cylinder, two-stroke

POWER:

22 kW (30 hp) at 7,500 rpm

DISPLACEMENT:

247 CC

PRODUCTION:

1973–1979

YAMAHA
RD 250

TECH SPECS

ENGINE:

Two-cylinder, two-stroke

POWER:

29 kW (39 hp) at 7,500 rpm

DISPLACEMENT:

347 cc

PRODUCTION:

1973–1979

Both the Yamaha RD 350 and its smaller sibling, the RD 250, seemed like a good choice for novice riders. After all, a smaller capacity meant they'd be cheaper and especially easy to handle, right? Wrong. What they didn't know was the handling characteristics of these bikes were erratic, if not downright scary: Powered by high-speed two-stroke engines, both bikes belied the fact that they were enormously fast by running deceptively slow at low rpm's, only to burst forth with a vengeance at high rpm's. This led to numerous accidents compelling Yamaha to slash engine power on these siblings.

Die RD 350 und ihre kleine Schwester RD 250 waren natürlich beliebt bei Fahranfängern. Eine kleine Hubraumzahl war nicht nur günstig, sondern versprach auch bequemes Handling. Doch hier irrte der Käufer. Die beiden Schwestern wucherten in den Fahreigenschaften mit einem hohen Zickenfaktor: Sie waren enorm schnell, aber entfalteten ihr Temperament als hochdrehende Zweitakter unterrum trügerisch langsam, bei höheren Drehzahlen dafür gewaltig. Ein Problem, das zu zahlreichen Unfällen führte und Yamaha später veranlasste, die Motoren zu drosseln.

YAMAHA
RD 350

TECH SPECS

ENGIINE:

Four-cylinder, four-stroke

POWER:

81 kW (110 hp) at 10,500 rpm

DISPLACEMENT:

749 CC

PRODUCTION:

1985–1991

YAMAHA
FZ 750 *(Genesis)*

A super athlete turned superstar. The moment was right. Yamaha's concept of utilizing four cylinders each equipped with five valves, distributing weights throughout the belly and frame of this machine essentially left any competition in the dust: The Yamaha FZ 750 became the first mass-produced motorbike with a 750-cc capacity to produce more than 100 hp along with a top speed north of 150 mph. It's a statement that resonates to this day.

Ein Supersportler als Superstar, zumindest seiner Zeit. Die Idee von Yamaha im Jahr 1984, vier Zylinder zu benutzen und fünf Ventile pro Zylinder arbeiten zu lassen, Gewichte im Bauch und am Skelett des Boliden zu verlagern, trieben die Maschine beeindruckend an sämtlichen Konkurrenten vorbei: Als erstes Serienbike mit über 100 PS aus 750 cm³ überschritt sie den 150-Meilen-(241,4 km/h)-Rubikon. Ein Statement, das bis heute nachhallt.

In the mid-1980s, the Japanese reigned supreme in motorcycle sports, having run all over their European competitors. Sales profits were going through the roof and things couldn't be better in the Land of the Rising Sun. Not surprisingly, their engineers were encouraged to push motorcycle design ever closer to its limits. In 1984, the RD 500 was primarily aimed at beating the two-stroke lineup of Suzuki and Kawasaki—and it did. What made the RD 500 better is that Yamaha took all its experience gained from the racetracks and conveyed it onto the streets virtually uncompromised. But a two-stroke is still a two-stroke, and an RD is an RD. Anybody wanting to ride one first needs to understand that the RD plays to a different beat—actually, three of 'em. At low rpm's, the RD seems at first to slow waltz, then casually break into a foxtrot before hitting the high rpm range. That's when it decides to play Speed Metal now!

Mitte der Achtzigerjahre waren die Japaner unter sich: Im Rennsport fuhren sie die Europäer in Grund und Boden, bei den Verkaufszahlen schwebten sie in Nippons Himmel. So war es kein Wunder, dass die Entwicklungen immer gewagtere Formen annahmen. Die RD 500 sollte 1984 vor allem die Zweitakter von Suzuki und Kawasaki in Schach halten – was sie auch tat. Denn Yamaha machte es hier besser: Sie übersetzten die Erfahrungen der Rennserie nahezu verlustfrei auf die Straße. Aber ein Zweitakter ist ein Zweitakter, und eine RD ist eine RD. Die Leistungsentfaltung – sie erforderte den musikalischen Piloten, der mit hohen Motor-Drehzahlen umzugehen weiß: Untenrum tanzte die RD Walzer, in der Mitte einen flotten Fox, aber kurz vor dem roten Bereich Speed Metal.

TECH SPECS

ENGINE:

Four-cylinder, two-stroke

POWER:

65 kW (88 hp) at 7,500 rpm

DISPLACEMENT:

499 CC

PRODUCTION:

1984–1987

YAMAHA
RD 500

YAMAHA
XS 1100

TECH SPECS

ENGINE:

Four-cylinder, four-stroke

POWER:

70 kW (95 hp) at 8,500 rpm

DISPLACEMENT:

1,100 cc

PRODUCTION:

1978–1983

Competitors couldn't seem to wrap their heads around it fast enough. Yamaha's newest ride weighed in at almost 640 pounds minus occupants and took 13 seconds to reach a top speed of 112 mph. BMW and domestic competitors alike were left in the dust by it. It was only the original suspension that didn't sit well with this fast lady. Once it hit 100 mph, it would express its dismay by precariously wobbling at the back end. Despite its quirks and twists, today the XS 1100 from 1978 is deemed to be the mother of all standard-made big bikes, its perfect shock absorbers making it pre-destined for long runs on which it offers plenty of room for luggage and, of course, for the passenger.

Die Konkurrenz war auf 180. Aber bei Weitem nicht so schnell wie die neue Kardan-Maschine von Yamaha, die ihre knapp 290 kg plus Fahrer in 13 Sekunden auf diese Geschwindigkeit schob. BMW und die japanischen Kollegen guckten in den Auspuff des Vierzylinder-Bikes. Das erste Fahrwerk war allerdings noch nicht ganz nach dem Geschmack der flotten Dame: Als Zeichen ihrer Verstimmtheit wackelte sie ab 160 km/h bedenklich mit dem Hintern. Heute sagt man, die XS 1100 von 1978 ist trotz jener Divenanfälle die Mutter aller Serien-Big-Bikes, perfekt in der Federung, prädestiniert für Longruns mit viel Platz für Gepäck und Beifahrer.

Even the predecessor had pretty outrageous power: 187 hp, 115 Newton meters of torque. But in times of a BMW S 1000 RR, certain basic points have to be answered, and so we have the new R1 with a completely new crossplane in-line four-cylinder engine, which, like the BMW competitor, now also comes in with 200 hp. To keep everything under control, there's a sensor cluster that electronically scans all of the bike's data and helps control traction, slide, wheelie, and braking.

Schon die Vorgängerin war brachial: 187 PS, 115 Newtonmeter Drehmoment. Doch in Zeiten einer BMW S 1000 RR gilt es eben, auch gewisse Grundsatzfragen zu beantworten, und so kommt die neue R1 mit einem komplett neuen Crossplane-Reihenvierzylinder-Motor, der, wie die BMW-Konkurrenz, jetzt ebenfalls mit 200 PS antritt. Um das alles im Zaum halten zu können, gibt es einen Sensorcluster, der das Bike elektronisch komplett abtastet und hilft, Traktion, Schlupf, Wheelie-Neigung und Bremsen zu kontrollieren.

TECH SPECS

ENGINE:

Four-cylinder in-line

POWER:

147 kW (200 hp) at 13,500 rpm

DISPLACEMENT:

998 cc

YAMAHA
YZF-R1

KENNY ROBERTS, SR.

THE BIKES – OUR HEROES · USA

Given the fact that nicknames are as much a part of motorcycle racing as burned out tires and fractured bones, Kenny Roberts Sr. has his own—"Big Mouth Roberts." It's certainly not the kind of nickname the California native would've had in mind back in 1978 when he kicked off the Motorcycle World Championship by announcing to the whole world that his goal was to win the Championship title; nothing more, nothing less. And sure enough: Racing on his Yamaha, he was soon trouncing the competition on a regular basis, clinching the Championship title three times in a row by 1980. In particular, Roberts became known for his "un-European" riding style, which he had developed while racing in the AMA Grand National Championship. Here, competitors didn't race on paved road circuits so much as on dirt tracks, sand-surfaced oval tracks, as well as sand-surfaced tracks including jumping hills. Winners and losers are determined first and foremost by their cornering skills, which Roberts had more than plenty of. Against this background, Roberts's racing style ultimately helped him win the World Championship and thus enter the league of kings of motorcycle racing. Next thing you know, *poof!* And he was no longer "Big Mouth Roberts" or "yellow midget" to certain circles of European motor racing community, no sir! From that point onward, Roberts was "King Kenny."

Weil Spitznamen in der Szene so normal sind wie Reifenverschleiß und Knochenbrüche, hat auch Kenny Roberts senior einen: „Großmaul Roberts". Zugegeben, der Kalifornier hätte sich 1978 sicherlich einen anderen gewünscht, verkündete allerdings schon vor der Motorradweltmeisterschaft, dass sein Ziel der Gewinn des Titels sei. Nicht mehr und nicht weniger. Fortan fuhr er auf Yamaha seiner Konkurrenz auf und davon und holte sich bis 1980 dreimal in Folge den Titel. Seinen „uneuropäischen" Fahrstil eignete sich Roberts während der AMA Grand National Championship an. Dabei ging es nämlich nicht nur auf Asphalt voran, sondern vielmehr auf Dirt-Track-Strecken, Sandovalen und Sandbahnen mit Sprunghügeln. Da muss man schon wissen, wann man sich wie in die Kurve legt. Er wusste es. Und siegte nicht zuletzt dank seines Stils in der Königsklasse. *Zack!* Schon war er nicht mehr das „Großmaul Roberts" oder der „Gelbe Zwerg" in der europäischen Rennszene. Roberts war fortan „King Kenny".

Originally, he just wanted to stay home and play some rock 'n' roll. Give him some drumsticks, a drum set, and success would be his, he figured. Well, success was his, all right. Except, it didn't come from handling some drumsticks and a drum set. Instead, it came from cracking the gas throttle of a motorbike. Randy Mamola was twelve years old when he decided to abandon drumming in favor of motorcycle racing. It was at a small track owned by the local Police Athletic League, just around the corner from his parents' home, where he rode his first motorbike. Soon he was racing in local events and, before long, he won the trophy as fastest junior rider in California. Securing the sponsorship of Yamaha, Randy Mamola first sealed the deal when he was fourteen. Sporting the colors of his idol, Kenny Roberts Senior, soon earned him the nickname "Baby Kenny." It's a somewhat comical nickname for a man who has started in the AMA 250 Championship, raced for Bimota, Honda, Suzuki, and Yamaha, and who won the Vice World Championship four times between 1980 and 1987. As a drummer, he surely would've admired John Bonham, but "Baby John?" That's OTL.

Eigentlich wollte er zu Hause so richtig Krach machen. Mit Drumsticks auf Trommeln dreschen, Musik machen, Erfolg haben. Das mit dem Erfolg hat super geklappt. Nur eben nicht mit den Sticks in der Hand, sondern dem Gashahn auf „Attacke". Randy Mamola fällte die Entscheidung gegen das Schlagzeug und für Motorradrennen bereits als 12-Jähriger. Quasi um die Ecke seines Elternhauses fuhr er auf dem Kurs einer Polizeisportanlage umher. Es folgen kleinere Rennen und die Auszeichnung als schnellster Nachwuchsfahrer in Kalifornien. Mit Yamaha als Sponsor zog Mamola schon als 14-Jähriger einen dicken Fisch an Land. Weil er Rennen in den Farben seines Idols Kenny Roberts sr. fuhr, gab man ihm den Spitznamen „Baby Kenny". Irgendwie witzig für jemanden, der in der AMA 250 Championship startete, Meisterschaftszweiter wurde, für Bimota in Daytona startete, Suzuki fuhr, Yamaha ins Ziel brachte und viermal Vize-Weltmeister wurde. Wäre er Drummer geworden, hätte er sicher John Bonham bewundert. Aber „Baby John"? Na ja.

 # RANDY MAMOLA

THE BIKES — OUR HEROES · USA

TECH SPECS

ENGINE:

Parallel twin

POWER:

82 kW (112 hp) at 7,250 rpm

DISPLACEMENT:

1,199 CC

YAMAHA

XT 1200 Z Super Ténéré ABS

Travel equals variety. And so Yamaha has appropriately stepped in with its long-distance tourer with adjustable chassis, good directional stability, and a super fine engine. Numerous carbon components and guards, revised drive modifications, a four-way adjustable windshield, a new cockpit plus GPS mount and gear display, cruise control, LED turn signals, and many other enhanced features mean that the XT is equipped for thrilling adventures around the world.

Reisen bedeutet Veränderung. Und so legte Yamaha ordentlich Hand an bei seinem Langstreckentourer mit einstellbarem Fahrwerk, gutem Geradeauslauf und einem äußerst feinem Motor. Zahlreiche Karbonteile und Protektoren, überarbeitete Fahrmodifikationen, ein vierfach verstellbares Windschild, ein neues Cockpit samt Navi-Halterung und Ganganzeige, Tempomat, LED-Blinker und zahlreiche weitere Verbesserungen rüsten die XT für neue Abenteuer rund um die Welt.

As a member of the sport heritage category, the XJR 1300 was almost an obvious choice for individual re-modeling. As an air-cooled big bike with a torque of 108 Newton meters, it's long been considered a classic. That's also underlined by the fact that, at the front, there is still no ABS, but four piston brake calipers. Thanks to Öhlins shocks at the back of the aluminum swing-arm, however, the 132-mph bike ensures a good road position in almost all situations.

Als Mitglied der Kategorie Sport Heritage drängt sich die XJR 1300 für den Individualumbau nahezu auf. Als luftgekühltes Big Bike mit 108 Newtonmeter Drehmoment gilt es sowieso schon seit Längerem als Klassiker, was auch dadurch unterstrichen wird, dass vorne noch ohne ABS, aber mit vier Kolben-Bremszangen zugepackt wird. Dank Öhlins-Dämpfer hinten an der Alu-Schwinge aber bietet das 213 km/h schnelle Bike eine gute Straßenlage in nahezu allen Situationen.

TECH SPECS

ENGINE:

Four-cylinder in-line

POWER:

72 kW (98 hp) at 8,000 rpm

DISPLACEMENT:

1,251 cc

YAMAHA
XJR 1300

Facing a mighty engine, the biker's seating position is like being enthroned inside a road cruiser. What sounds like a typical 1970s American cruiser, is in fact a comfortable 750-pound bike, which is stable and relaxing to drive, thanks to a superb quality chassis. To ensure that this amount of weight can also be safely brought to a halt, the brakes work with an integrated system that also stops the front wheel with the foot.

Ein gewaltiger Motor sitzt vor dem Fahrer, der in der optischen Verpackung eines Straßenkreuzers thront. Was klingt wie ein typischer Ami aus den Siebzigerjahren, ist in Wahrheit ein komfortables Bike mit 340 kg, das sich dank souveränem Fahrwerk stabil und entspannt dirigieren lässt. Damit diese Masse aber auch ebenso sicher wieder zum Stehen kommt, arbeiten die Bremsen mithilfe eines Integralsystems, das mit dem Fuß das Vorderrad mit abbremst.

TECH SPECS

ENGINE:

V2

POWER:

66 kW (90 hp) at 4,750 rpm

DISPLACEMENT:

1,854 cc

YAMAHA
XV 1900 A

TECH SPECS

ENGINE:

V4

POWER:

147 kW (200 hp) at 9,000 rpm

DISPLACEMENT:

1,679 cc

YAMAHA
Vmax

There's one thing that the Vmax is not, and one thing that it never wants to be, namely, an entry-level bike: 200 hp and a torque of 160 Newton meters deliver a message that makes even an 8-inch rear tire show the strain. The V4 engine has been developed exclusively for this model and works with variable intakes and electronically controlled throttle valves. The air for the engine is collected through large ducts. The radial mount brakes with ABS slow everything down again.

Eines ist die Vmax nicht und eines wollte sie nie sein: eine Einsteigermaschine. 200 PS und 160 Newtonmeter Drehmoment sind eine Ansage, bei der sogar ein 200er-Hinterreifen ernsthaft ins Schwitzen kommt. Der V4 wurde ausschließlich für dieses Modell entwickelt und arbeitet mit variablen Ansaugstutzen und elektronisch geregelten Drosselklappen. Für die für den Motor notwendige Luft sorgen gewaltige Hutzen. Eingefangen wird alles wieder von den radial angeschlagenen Bremsen mit ABS.

EGON MÜLLER

They used to call him "Rocket Müller," and for good reason: When starting, Egon Müller would quite literally launch like a rocket, which is the key to success in Speedway Racing. The trick is to lean into the very first turn and to make sure nobody passes you. Indeed, Egon Müller was very successful at it. To this day, he remains the only German to ever become Speedway World Champion. However, his 33-year career went beyond that. Between 1974 and 1978, Müller won the European Championship three times on the long course; between 1970 and 1985, he clinched 5 German Speedway Championship titles, he set up a new world record at the Grasbahn European Championship in Germany, celebrated 36 new records on the race track as well as 785 racing victories. Think success through willpower. And hard work. That's because Müller trained like a madman while working just as intensely on his bike. Having put everything on the line, not even bone fractures, of which he suffered a total of 67 throughout his career, kept him from going to the start. The fact that Egon Müller could be regarded as a living, breathing synthesis of the arts is in part due to his career outside of the dirt track. It's not unusual for him to grab a mike and start crooning hits like "Rock & Rollin' Speedway Man" or "The Devil Wins." Chances are, the devil never went face-to-face with "Rocket Müller."

Sie nannten ihn „Raketen-Müller". Nicht ohne Grund: Beim Start ging Egon Müller im wahrsten Sinne des Wortes raketenmäßig ab. Was bei Speedway-Rennen der Schlüssel zum Erfolg ist. Ab in die erste Kurve und keinen mehr vorbeilassen. Und ja, Egon Müller hatte Erfolg. Er ist bis heute der einzige Deutsche, der Weltmeister im Speedway wurde. Dabei blieb es aber nicht in seiner 33-jährigen Karriere: Zwischen 1974 und 1978 wurde Müller dreimal Weltmeister auf der Langbahn, von 1970 bis 1985 errang er 5 deutsche Meistertitel im Speedway, er stellte einen Weltrekord auf der Grasbahn auf, feierte 36 Bahnrekorde und 785 Rennsiege. Ein Erfolg durch Willensstärke. Und Fleiß. Denn Müller trainierte wie ein Besessener und schraubte ebenso intensiv an seiner Maschine. Wenn es um alles ging, hielten ihn auch Knochenbrüche, von denen er in seiner Karriere 67 an der Zahl erlitt, nicht davon ab, an den Start zu gehen. Dass man Egon Müller auch als Gesamtkunstwerk bezeichnen kann, liegt auch an seiner Karriere neben der Sandbahn: Da griff er gerne mal zum Mikrofon und sang Hits wie „Rock & Rollin' Speedway Man" oder „The Devil Wins". Nur hat der Teufel vermutlich nicht mit dem Raketen-mann gerechnet.

"There's no such thing as a slow bike, only slow riders."

Valentino Rossi

„Es gibt keine langsamen Motorräder, nur langsame Fahrer."

Valentino Rossi

HAVING A PROPER BIKE, ALL YOU NEED IS A DESTINATION– MAINLY, THE ROAD. OF COURSE, YOU DON'T WANT JUST ANY ROAD. YOU CAN TAKE ROUTE 66, WHICH IS ALWAYS WORTH THE TRIP. EXCEPT THERE ARE SO MANY OTHER PLACES TO EXPLORE TOO. BESIDES, IF THERE'S ONE THING A BIKER LIKES MORE THAN RIDING HIS BIKE ALONE, IT'S BEING IN THE COMPANY OF FELLOW BIKERS. HEADING OUT INTO THE GREAT WIDE OPEN, THERE'S A REAL CHANCE TO HOOK UP WITH SOME KINDRED SPIRITS ALONG THE WAY. WHERE? AT BIKER MEETS AND RALLIES, OF COURSE.

MIT DER RICHTIGEN MASCHINE KANN ES NUR EIN ZIEL GEBEN – DIE STRASSE. ES SOLLTE NATÜRLICH DIE RICHTIGE STRASSE SEIN. DIE ROUTE 66 WÄRE DA EINE REISE WERT. ES GIBT ABER NOCH SEHR VIEL MEHR ZU ENTDECKEN. UND DA EIN MOTORRADFAHRER ZWAR GERNE ALLEIN AUF SEINEM BIKE SITZT, ABER GEMEINSAM IM PULK FÄHRT, BIETET SICH AUF DER REISE GEGEN DAS FERNWEH SO WUNDERBAR GESELLSCHAFT AN. MAN KANN SICH DOCH MIT NOCH MEHR GLEICHGESINNTEN TREFFEN. WO? NA, BEI BIKER-TREFFEN.

Where Passion Is Experienced

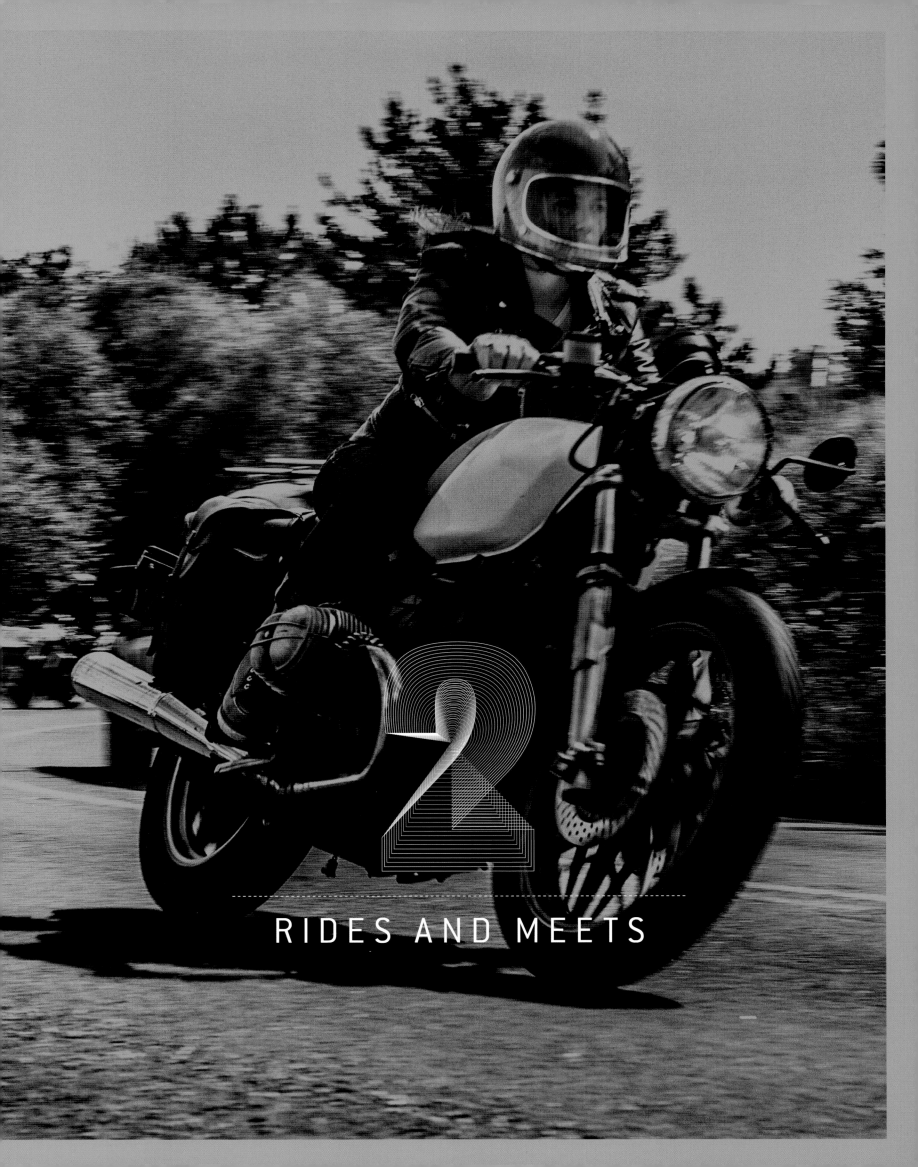

2

RIDES AND MEETS

Route 66 –
The Mother Road
for Bikers

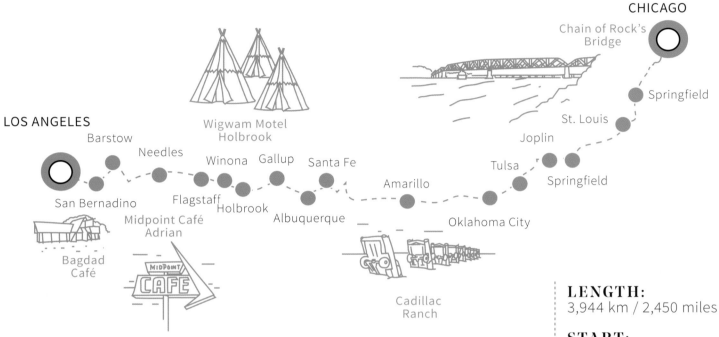

LOS ANGELES

Barstow
Needles
Winona
Gallup
Santa Fe

Wigwam Motel
Holbrook

CHICAGO

Chain of Rock's
Bridge

Springfield

St. Louis

Joplin

Tulsa

Springfield

Amarillo

San Bernadino

Flagstaff
Holbrook
Albuquerque

Oklahoma City

Midpoint Café
Adrian

Bagdad
Café

Cadillac
Ranch

UNITED STATES
OF AMERICA

LENGTH:
3,944 km / 2,450 miles

START:
Chicago (Illinois)

FINISH:
Santa Monica (California)

TOP TIPS:

- CHAIN OF ROCK'S BRIDGE NEAR MADISON (ILLINOIS)
- WIGWAM MOTEL IN HOLBROOK (ARIZONA)
- MIDPOINT CAFÉ IN ADRIAN (TEXAS)
- CADILLAC RANCH NEAR AMARILLO (TEXAS)
- BAGDAD CAFÉ FEATURED IN THE FILM *OUT OF ROSENHEIM* IN BAGDAD (CALIFORNIA)

For more information visit:
www.historic66.com

It's a weird paradox: Following an ugly fall into neglect, this world-famous route pulled off one impressive comeback. That's exactly how bikers like to see it. This 2,450-mile route from Chicago to Santa Monica, California, was originally one of the first continuous stretches of highway linking Chicago directly with the West Coast. At some point, the amount of traffic got crazy. As the decades went by, five new interstate highways were built to relieve the strain: Route 66 seemed like a forgotten world of cities, villages, roadside truck stops, and restaurants cast into oblivion. True, they kept their original 1930s and 1940s charm—that was the heyday of Route 66 eternalized in Bobby Troup's song "Get Your Kicks on Route Sixty Six." Nowadays, that same old charm works its magic on tourists and nostalgia enthusiasts from all walks of life. But easy riders shouldn't be deterred: Route 66 remains the Mother Road for all bikers.

Ihr Niedergang verhalf ihr zum Comeback. Hört sich paradox an, aus Bikersicht ist das aber haargenau zutreffend. Ursprünglich war die knapp viertausend Kilometer lange Strecke zwischen Chicago und dem kalifornischen Santa Monica eine der ersten durchgehend befestigten Straßenverbindungen zur US-amerikanischen Westküste. Irgendwann wurde der Verkehr zu viel für die Straße, im Laufe der Jahrzehnte übernahmen fünf neue Interstate-Highways ihre Funktion. Die Route 66 geriet in Vergessenheit, ebenso die Städte und Dörfer, die Truck Stops und Restaurants – und behielten somit ihren Charme aus den Dreißiger- und Vierzigerjahren, als die Strecke ihre Blütezeit hatte und in Bobby Troups „Get Your Kicks on Route Sixty Six" besungen wurde. Genau dieser Charme lockt heute Nostalgiker und Touristen aller Art an – was echte Easy Rider nicht stören sollte, ist die Route 66 doch die Mutter aller Biker-Routen.

ALPS

The Alps – Cruising from Pass to Pass

SWITZERLAND

Rhône Glacier

Aletschhorn

FRANCE

Chamonix

Col du
Galibier   Mont Blanc

Aosta

Briançon

Andermatt

Matterhorn

Lugano

Lake
Maggiore

Galtür   Kühtai

Livigno

St. Moritz

Klobenstein

SEEFELD

Krimml
Waterfalls

Lake Garda

AUSTRIA

Kaprun

Grossglockner

Dolomites

ITALY

LENGTH:
3,250 km / 2,020 miles

START / FINISH:
Seefeld (Austria)

TOP TIPS:

- KRIMML WATERFALLS /
  HOHE TAUERN (AUSTRIA)

- MATTERHORN /
  CANTON VALAIS (SWITZERLAND)

- RHÔNE GLACIER /
  CANTON VALAIS (SWITZERLAND)

- MONT BLANC / HAUTE-SAVOIE
  (FRANCE)

- TRE CIME / DOLOMITES /
  SOUTH TYROL (ITALY)

For more information visit:
www.edelweissbike.com

At least once in a lifetime, any self-respecting biker should have cruised up the high-altitude Stelvia Pass in Italy. Oh, you're not convinced by the 87 serpentine bends? You could practice cornering to dizzy perfection before the fabulous ride across the Alpine Mountain range. Take it gently to start off in Seefeld, Tyrol, Austria. Then, head in a westerly direction over the Kühtai Saddle toward the Silvretta High Alpine Road, through the principality of Liechtenstein, onward to Switzerland's Klausen and Furka Passes, past the Rhône glacier, Aletschhorn, and Matterhorn. Continue into France, past Mont Blanc, and climb the Tour de France passes like the Col du Galibier. Next head eastward: Ride via Aosta Valley, Lake Maggiore, the San Bernadino Pass, St. Moritz, the Ofen Pass. Then, take the Stelvia Pass into the Dolomites over the Großglockner High Alpine Road and Kaprun, Austria, back to your starting point in Seefeld.

Eines ist sicher: Wer als Biker etwas auf sich hält, der sollte mindestens einmal in Leben das Stilfser Joch hochgecruist sein. Falls überzeugende Argumente benötigt werden, sollten 87 (!) Serpentinen reichen. Derart geübt, lässt sich dann gleich der ganze Alpenbogen durchfahren. Wir fangen ganz gemächlich an in Seefeld, Tirol. Über den Kühtai-Sattel geht es in Richtung Westen zu Silvretta-Hochalpenstraße, durch das Fürstentum Liechtenstein hindurch zum Klausen- und Furkapass in der Schweiz, vorbei an Rhonegletscher, Aletschhorn und Matterhorn. Dann weiter nach Frankreich, vorbei am Mont Blanc und hoch auf die Pässe der Tour de France wie den Col du Galibier. Und dann geht's wieder zurück nach Osten: über das Aosta-Tal, Lago Maggiore, San-Bernadino-Pass, St. Moritz, Ofenpass und das Stilfser Joch hinein in die Dolomiten, über die Großglockner-Hochalpenstraße und Kaprun zurück zum Ausgangspunkt nach Seefeld.

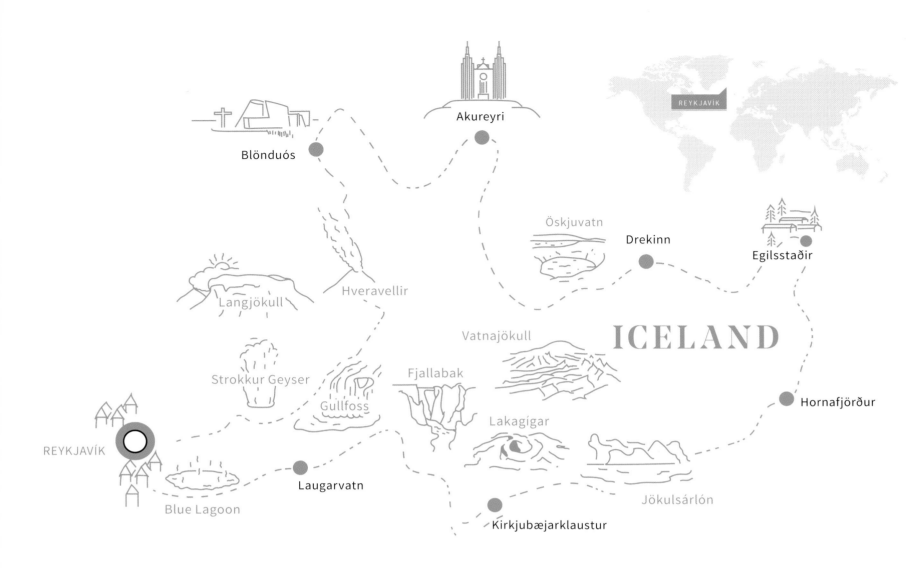

Blönduós

Akureyri

REYKJAVÍK

Öskjuvatn

Drekinn

Egilsstaðir

Hveravellir

Langjökull

Vatnajökull

ICELAND

Strokkur Geyser

Fjallabak

Gullfoss

Lakagígar

Hornafjörður

REYKJAVÍK

Laugarvatn

Jökulsárlón

Blue Lagoon

Kirkjubæjarklaustur

ICELAND
Fire and Ice

Some say Iceland is just an island. Instead, let's settle for an adventure playground! The land of boiling mud pools, hissing and spitting geysers, incredible glaciers, and magical legends: Iceland has waterfalls, and volcanoes, of course. But Iceland is also Europe's most sparsely populated nation. Half of the country's 320,000 residents live in the capital, Reykjavík, leaving the island's 40,000 square miles of extensive uninhabited territory as an awesome space for a motorcycle expedition. The ride starts in the capital city and vanguard of culture, Reykjavík. It continues into the northern highlands, past geysers and waterfalls, and to the famous roads like the Hringvegur Ring Road. At Akureyri, in the far north, the journey carries on to Vatnajökull National Park; it's a lonesome off-road run to Europe's biggest glacier—the Jökulsárlón—and then back again to the Ring Road. This tracks along the south coast to Svartifoss, the black waterfall. After another detour through the highlands, it's straight back to the Blue Lagoon, which is like a gigantic bathtub spread over 55,000 square feet where the water temperature rises to between 98 and 107 °F. Take it easy and park the bike here for a while.

Manche nennen es Insel. Andere sagen Island dazu. Wir nennen es einfach Abenteuerspielplatz. Es ist das Land der kochenden Schlammpfühle, der spuckenden Geysire, der mächtigen Gletscher und der magischen Sagen. Wasserfälle gibt's auch. Vulkane sowieso. Vor allem aber ist es das am dünnsten besiedelte Land Europas. Von den 320.000 Einwohnern des Landes wohnt die Hälfte in der Hauptstadt Rejkjavík, sodass der große Rest sich perfekt mit dem Motorrad ausfüllen lässt. Die Tour startet in der Hauptstadt und Kulturhochburg Reykjavík. Es geht ins nördliche Hochland, vorbei an Geysiren und Wasserfällen auf die berühmteste Straße des Landes, dem Hringvegur – der Ringstraße. Ganz im Norden in Akureyri angekommen, geht's der Südküste entlang nach Svartifoss, dem schwarzen Wasserfall, und zur Blauen Lagune, so einer Art riesigen Badewanne mit einer Fläche von 5000 m² und einer Wassertemperatur von 37 bis 42 °C. Dafür lässt man dann auch mal sein Bike stehen.

LENGTH:
2,000 km / 1,250 miles

START / FINISH:
Reykjavík (Iceland)

TOP TIPS:
- HAUKADALUR, HOT SPRING AND GEOTHERMAL AREA
- GULLFOSS WATERFALL
- THINGVELLIR, SITE OF THE ALTHING, FORMER OPEN-AIR ASSEMBLY IN THINGVELLIR NATIONAL PARK
- JÖKULSÁRLÓN, EUROPE'S LARGEST GLACIER LAKES
- THE BLUE LAGOON NEAR GRINDAVÍK

For more information visit:
www.edelweissbike.com

A Zigzag Run Across the Fifth Continent

Broome

Coral Bay

Shark Bay

Karijini National Park

Alice Springs

Ayers Rock

AUSTRALIA

Wilpena Pound

Twelve Apostles

PERTH

SYDNEY

Melbourne

Opera House
Sydney

LENGTH:
10,500 km / 6,500 miles

START:
Perth (Western Australia)

FINISH:
Sydney (New South Wales)

TOP TIPS:

- KARIJINI NATIONAL PARK:
  KEEP COOL IN THE WATERHOLES

This ride takes us into the Blue Mountains. No kidding! The Blue Mountains—one of the wonders of the fifth continent—earn their name from the eucalyptus leaves that release droplets of eucalyptus oil to create a misty blue haze in daylight. You get the same effect, just more easily, by burning off some gas; so, wait for the blue mist to rise. We did that, though we began from the other end of Australia, in Perth, on the West Coast. With the Indian Ocean in view, head for Coral Bay, where you can greet ocean turtles and giant manta ray before visiting the pearling tourist town of Broome. Then head north for the Kakadu National Park, one of Australia's most beautiful destinations, and not entirely without natural hazards, because—the clue's in the name—this park is within the Alligator Rivers Region. Next, we turn south to Ayers Rock via the Great Ocean Road to Sydney and into the Blue Mountains. You should be careful: This region's scorching hot! Take the local advice about staying alert for kangaroos on the road, plus other hazards, like 230-foot long road trains that thunder along the highway.

Zu den Blauen Bergen fahren wir. Kein Scherz! Sondern einer der Höhepunkte des Fünften Kontinents. Die Blue Mountains verdanken ihren Namen den Blättern des Eukalyptus. Diese verdunsten ein ätherisches Öl, dessen feiner Nebel wiederum das Tageslicht bricht und so einen blauen Schimmer erzeugt. Das geht natürlich auch etwas einfacher, indem man Benzin verdunstet und auf eine ebensolche Lichtbrechung hofft. Gesagt, getan, wir starten am entgegengesetzten Ende Australiens, an der Westküste in Perth. Am Indischen Ozean entlang geht's nach Coral Bay, wo, wer will, den Meeresschildkröten und Riesenmantas ein „Hello" zuwerfen kann, bevor es weiter geht in die Perlenstadt Broome und nach Norden in den Kakadu-Nationalpark. Er ist einer der schönsten Australiens und nicht ganz so harmlos, wie der Name vermuten lässt, schließlich befindet er sich in der Alligator Rivers Region. Dann ab nach Süden am Ayers Rock, vorbei über die Great Ocean Road nach Sydney und in die Blauen Berge. Aber Achtung: Es wird heiß, Kängurus könnten im Weg stehen und mehr als 70 Meter lange Road Trains rocken die Straßen.

- SHARK BAY: SPEAR FISHING
  WITH ABORIGINAL PEOPLE
- WILPENA POUND IN FLINDERS
  RANGES NATIONAL PARK:
  A MASSIVE, NATURAL
  AMPHITHEATER OF MOUNTAINS
- SYDNEY OPERA HOUSE
- TWELVE APOSTLES BETWEEN
  PRINCETOWN AND PORT CAMPBELL

For more information visit:
www.edelweissbike.com

Rico:

"I'm freakin pumped!

I've been drinking green tea all day!"

From the movie
Hot Rod

Rico:

„Ich bin auf 180!

Ich trinke schon den ganzen Tag grünen Tee!"

Aus dem Film
*Hot Rod – Mit Vollgas
durch die Hölle*

The Distinguished Gentleman's Ride

It's not essential to be that smartly dressed for this ride. But a Louis Vuitton suit, white shirt, cuffs, and necktie plus shiny boots will do nicely for participating in the gentlemen's gathering of bikers to cruise around downtown. You can also don classic leather gloves and suitable helmet. The Distinguished Gentleman's Ride is a festival for dapper riders on two wheels—preferably on classic style motorcycles. Bikers taking part here help to raise money for a cure for prostate cancer. This annual worldwide event is held on the last weekend in September. In 2012, the first meet already attracted over 2,500 riders in 64 cities around the world. In 2014, the phenomenon spread across 220 cities, with 20,000 riders kick-starting their machines. You'll be welcomed if you dust off classic gentlemen's attire, but starting on the right motorcycle is also important: A café racer, bobber, a custom or classic bike—any of these will do. Why not sport designer stubble, or even full and fine whiskers? That'll be about right to be in this league.

Nein, für dieses Treffen braucht man sich nicht übermäßig in Schale zu werfen, ein Louis-Vuitton-Anzug mit schlichtem, weißem Button-up-Shirt, Krawatte, aufgeschlagene Ärmel und auf Hochglanz polierte Schuhe reichen völlig aus, um als Gentleman im Pulk durch die Stadt zu cruisen. Klassische Lederhandschuhe dürfen natürlich auch gerne getragen werden, der passende Helm sowieso. Der Distinguished Gentleman's Ride ist ein Fest der Eleganz auf zwei – möglichst klassischen – Rädern, bei dem per gemeinsamer Motorradfahrt Geld gesammelt für den Kampf gegen Prostatakrebs wird – und zwar weltweit, jeweils am letzten Septemberwochenende. Bereits die erste Ausfahrt versammelte 2012 mehr als 2500 Gentleman-Biker in 64 Städten weltweit. 2014 waren es bereits um die 20.000 in 220 Städten – Tendenz steigend. Wer mitfahren möchte, braucht nicht nur klassisch-elegante Kleidung, sondern auch das richtige Bike. Einen Café Racer zum Beispiel, einen Bobber, ein Custom Bike oder Classic Bike wäre angebracht. Ganz zeitgemäß darf auch ruhig ein wenig Gesichtsbehaarung sein, gerne auch mehr, wenn sie entsprechend elegant drapiert wird.

Where ?	Worldwide		Wo?	Weltweit
When ?	Annually, last weekend in September		Wann?	Letztes Wochenende im September
Who ?	Dapper riders on custom bikes, café racers, classic bikes, bobbers, and more		Wer?	Gut gekleidete Fahrer auf Custom Bikes, Café Racern, Classic Bikes, Bobbern und Ähnlichen
	www.gentlemansride.com			www.gentlemansride.com

Where ?	Thurmansbang-Solla/Loh in the middle of the Bavarian Forest, approx. 25 miles north of Passau (Germany)	Wo?	Thurmansbang-Solla/Loh im Bayerischen Wald, ca. 40 km nördlich von Passau (Deutschland)
When ?	End of January	Wann?	Ende Januar
Who ?	All bikers who own motorcycles suitable for snow and icy conditions www.bvdm.de/et.html	Wer?	Alle winterharten Biker mit schnee- und eistauglichen Bikes www.bvdm.de/et.html

Elefantentreffen

You've really got to want to be here—even as a hardened biker who braves all the elements. The Bavarian "Elefantentreffen" (Elephant Rally) is not so much about robust bikes, as it's about guaranteed snow. While other bikers store their machines safely in the garage through winter, every year 5,000 to 10,000 bikers from across Europe gather in the Bavarian Forest. It's here in the so-called "Witches' Cauldron," a deep valley between Loh, Solla, and Thurmansbang, not far from the Czech Republic, that crowds of fearless bikers camp out in the freezing wet snow. Despite January's usual cool temperatures, every biker who makes it here seems not to mind stripping semi-naked in the frosty conditions. Furthermore, the guidelines for street-legal practice, like fitting motorcycles with winter tires, seem to present only minor difficulties: These bikers are so determined to be in this ice ride that occasionally they arrive on "creative" custom builds. The rallies were a fixture for nearly sixty years—the first one was back in 1956, at the Solitude racetrack in Stuttgart. They transferred via the Nürburgring and Salzburgring to the site in the Bavarian Forest as late as 1989. By the way, the namesake for this event is the Zündapp KS 601. That was the machine for which the motorcycling journalist, Ernst Leverkus, originally started the rally: The KS 601's nickname is "green elephant."

Das muss man wirklich wollen – auch als hartgesottener, wetterfester Biker. Denn das Elefantentreffen legt weniger Wert auf dicke Bikes als vielmehr auf eine schneesichere Lage. Richtig verstanden: Schnee. Wenn andere ihre Bikes winterfest eingemottet haben, zieht es jährlich 5000 bis 10.000 Motorradfahrer aus ganz Europa in den Bayerischen Wald. Dort, in einem „Hexenkessel" betitelten Talkessel zwischen den Orten Loh, Thurmansbang und Solla nahe der tschechischen Grenze, treffen sich die Unerschrockenen zum gemeinsamen Massencampen in Matsch und Schnee – und lassen dort auch schon mal die Hüllen bis zur Halbnackigkeit fallen, ungeachtet der Temperaturen, die sich Ende Januar gerne mal im Minusbereich bewegen. Die Biker lassen sich auch von gesetzlichen Hürden wie der Winterreifenpflicht für Motorräder nicht von dem eisigen Vergnügen abhalten, sondern reisen teils mit durchaus kreativ zu nennenden Spezialkonstruktionen an. Seit gut sechzig Jahren gibt es das Treffen, erstmals fand es 1956 auf der Solitude-Rennstrecke in Stuttgart statt und wanderte über den Nürburgring und Salzburgring 1989 schließlich in den Bayerischen Wald. Seinen Namen verdankt das Treffen übrigens der Zündapp KS 601 – für dieses Gefährt hatte der Motorradjournalist Ernst Leverkus das Treffen ins Leben gerufen. Der Spitzname der KS 601 lautet nämlich „Grüner Elefant."

Wheels and Waves

There are just six of them. These six call themselves "Southsiders." They're passionate about motorcycles: classic bikes and café racers. Plus, they love their surfboards, too. And anything with a whiff of history that, nonetheless, is rooted in the present. A blog was the start of it all. In six short years, Wheels and Waves has become an international rally for bikers and surfers. This is a glorious celebration of the 1960s, when everybody felt a buzz about all machines on two wheels and for all sports using boards. Back then, there was a wonderful carefree atmosphere. So, it's no accident that this festival is about pushing the boundaries—car drivers with the right vehicle are welcome, and with the right attitude! Biking and surfing come top of the bill, but there are also exhibitions, concerts, and much more. One of the founding members, Vincent Prat, explains: "The reason for this event is the desire for freedom. And although that reveals a yearning for nostalgia, it's also about lost freedoms."

Sie sind sechs. Sie nennen sich Southsider. Sie lieben Motorräder. Alte Motorräder. Café Racer. Und sie lieben Surfbretter. Alles, was alt ist und trotzdem ganz im Heute verankert. Mit einem Blog hat es angefangen, zu einem internationalen Biker- und Surfertreffen ist Wheels and Waves in nur sechs Jahren angewachsen. Gefeiert werden hier vor allem die Sechzigerjahre, als die Begeisterung für alles Zweirädrige und alle Brettsportarten noch so etwas wie eine kindliche Unschuld umwehte. Es ist ein Festival, das gezielt Grenzen überschreitet – Autofahrer mit dem richtigen Gefährt und vor allem der richtigen Einstellung sind ebenso willkommen. Es wird nicht nur gebiket und gesurft, sondern es gibt auch Ausstellungen, Konzerte und und und. Vincent Prat, einer der Gründerväter, sagt dazu: „Bei diesem Event zählt allein der Wille zur Freiheit. Und ja, wenn das eine gewisse nostalgische Sehnsucht hervorruft, dann die nach verlorenen Freiheiten."

Where ?	Biarritz Beach in South West France	**Wo?**	Am Strand von Biarritz in Südwestfrankreich
When ?	In June	**Wann?**	Im Juni
Who ?	Anyone with vision beyond the handlebar	**Wer?**	Alle, die auch über den Lenker hinaus blicken
	www.wheels-and-waves.com		www.wheels-and-waves.com

Where ?	Glen Helen Raceway, San Bernardino, California (USA)	Wo?	Glen Helen Raceway, San Bernardino, Kalifornien (USA)
When ?	The boss decides the dates	Wann?	Je nach Laune des Chefs
Who?	Vintage bikers into fooling around more than competitive rally events	Wer?	Vintage-Biker, die Spaß dem Wettbewerb vorziehen
	www.hellonwheelsmc.com		www.hellonwheelsmc.com

Hell on Wheels
Halloween Hillclimb and other fun races

A few friendly guys and gals, a vintage dirt bike, quirky attire—what else do you need to have fun? We mean fiendishly good fun! That was the big idea of Jeff Tilinius—aka "Meatball" to those in the café racer scene—when he dreamed up the Halloween Hillclimb on the Glen Helen dirt track. His greatest worry was the possible arrival of a bona fide racing biker geared up to finish a strong competitive rally. Fortunately, nobody like that turned up. After all, the point was to relax, show off some wheelies, and bask in the spirit of the early 1970s when fun was the name of the game. Vintage was top of the agenda for the event. The same goes for all the runs that Tilinius regularly organizes under the "Hell on Wheels" brand. That's also the name of his vintage motorcycle shop in Anaheim, California. Hell on Wheels events also include the manic Whiskey Challenge, the Hot Summer Nights run, a rally open to bikers who could get to Japan, and finally the Day in the Dirt, when the dust flies at the Glen Helen track.

Ein paar Kumpel, ein Vintage Dirt Bike, eine lustige Verkleidung – mehr braucht man nicht, um Spaß zu haben. Um richtig Spaß zu haben. Das dachte sich zumindest Jeff Tulinius – in der Café-Racer-Szene besser bekannt als „Meatball" –, als er den Halloween Hillclimb auf dem Dirt Track von Glen Helen ausrief. Denn seine größte Sorge war wohl, dass tatsächlich ein echter Rennfahrer auftauchen würde, der ein ernsthaftes Rennen absolvieren will. Der kam aber nicht. Es geht ohnehin um lässiges Herumblödeln, und das im Geiste der frühen Siebziger, als der Spaß noch ganz klar vor allen Regularien im Vordergrund stand. Ohnehin, die ganze Veranstaltung ist auf Vintage poliert. So wie all die anderen Rennen auch, die Tulinius unter dem Gütesiegel „Hell on Wheels" – dem Namen seines Vintage-Motorcycle-Shops im kalifornischen Anaheim – immer wieder organisiert. Da gibt es die durchgeknallte Whiskey Challenge, die Hot Summer Nights, zwischendurch einen kleinen Ausflug nach Japan und zuletzt den Day in the Dirt, bei dem wieder die Strecke von Glen Helen umgepflügt wird. Alles unter dem Markenzeichen Hell on Wheels.

Motorcycle Film Festival

Founded in 2013, the Motorcycle Film Festival in New York City is a meeting point for independent filmmakers, garage artists, video bloggers, and bike paparazzi. Not to mention bikers themselves, who take an interest in all motorcycle models, sizes, and brands. For a while, they switch off their machines to watch other biker styles. The one-of-a-kind film festival celebrates the early 21st century as the era of the biggest creative boom in motorcycles since the 1970s: There are motorcycle customizers, video filmmakers, YouTube artists, and fabricator wizards. Nowadays, it's normal for every customizer to involve an in-house filmmaker, just as every hip biker event has a photographer. That's a good enough reason for a festival that selects 75 film works from a host of entries. As with other film festivals, the entrants compete to impress the jury. Prizes are awarded for the best feature documentary film, best short film, and best feature film. Jury members include biking royalty like bike designer Roland Sands. But at the heart of it all is a celebration of biking spirit.

Seit 2013 ist das Motorcycle Film Festival in New York City ein Treffpunkt für Independent-Filmmacher, Garagenkünstler, Video-Blogger und Bike-Paparazzi. Und natürlich von Bikern aller Typen, Größen und Marken. Die stellen ihre Maschinen mal ab, um anderen beim Biken zuzuschauen. Das Festival feiert so auf seine Weise, dass das beginnende 21. Jahrhundert die Ära des wohl größten kreativen Booms in der Zweiradwelt seit den Siebzigern ist, mit all den Custom-Bikern und Videofilmern, den YouTube- und Schraubkünstlern. Jeder Customizer hat heutzutage seinen In-House-Filmer, jedes hippe Motorrad-Event seine Fotografen. Genügend Stoff für ein Festival, das unter den unzähligen Einreichungen 75 Werke auswählt, die dann – wie es sich für ein Filmfestival gehört – um die Gunst der Jury streiten. Preise gibt's für den besten Dokumentarfilm, den besten Kurzfilm und den besten Spielfilm. In der Jury sitzen Szenegrößen wie der Rennfahrer und Bike-Designer Roland Sands. Vor allem aber geht es um den Spirit des Bikens.

Where ?	The Gutter Theater & Genuine Motorworks, North 14th Street, Brooklyn, New York City (USA)		**Wo?**	The Gutter & Genuine Motorworks, North 14th Street, Brooklyn, New York City (USA)
When ?	In September		**Wann?**	Im September
Who ?	Custom bikers		**Wer?**	Custom Biker
	www.motorcyclefilmfestival.com			www.motorcyclefilmfestival.com

Deus Slidetober Fest

Let's begin at the end...the end of the three-day Slidetober Fest on the island of Bali...a party that would delight Bacchus, the god of wine! According to organizers of the Indonesian branch of Australian custom bike and board maker, Deus Ex Machina, the day after the fest, participants are seen everywhere lying exhausted beneath Bali's palm trees. Well, it's worth it! First comes the party, then the surfing in the Wheel of Steel Surf Contest, and on the third day, time for the bikes to join in the Motocross Madness Contest on the dirt track in Denpasar. The kids get to go first on the track, then the ladies. The 225-cc class is next up at the starting line. The parade of vintage bikes is the absolute highlight. Anyone arriving without a bike—it's a hassle taking your moped on the plane—can borrow a Deus machine. The important point is to remember to return the bike in good time before Bacchus takes charge.

Fangen wir von hinten an: Am Ende des dreitägigen Slidetober-Fests auf Bali steigt nämlich eine Party, auf die Bacchus stolz wäre. Das betonen zumindest die Veranstalter von der indonesischen Dependance der australischen Custom-Bike-and-Board-Schmiede Deus Ex Machina. Und manch verknautschtes Partygänger-Gesicht soll am Tag danach unter Balis Palmen gesichtet worden sein. Aber gut, es lohnt sich ja schließlich. Erst wird gefeiert, dann beim Wheel of Steel Surf Contest gesurft, am dritten Tag schließlich geht's auf die Bikes zum Motocross Madness Contest auf dem Dirt Track von Denpasar. Erst dürfen die Kids auf die Strecke, dann die Frauen. Dann geht die 225 -cm³-Klasse an den Start, und als Höhepunkt werden die Vintage Bikes ausgepackt. Wer ohne Bike anreist – ist ja manchmal doch etwas umständlich, das Moped im Flugzeug mitzunehmen – kann sich eine Maschine bei Deus leihen. Aber nicht vergessen, das gute Stück rechtzeitig zurückzugeben, bevor Bacchus zu seinem Recht kommt.

Where ?	Canggu Beach, Bali (Indonesia)		**Wo?**	Canggu, Bali (Indonesien)
When ?	Mid-October		**Wann?**	Mitte Oktober
Who ?	Fun bikers and surfers		**Wer?**	Fun-Biker und Surfer
	www.deuscustoms.com/blog			www.deuscustoms.com/blog

Where ?	Ace Cafe, Stonebridge, London (UK)	Wo?	Ace Cafe, Stonebridge, London (GB)
When ?	Mid-September	Wann?	Mitte September
Who ?	Everyone who is able to quit using clichés	Wer?	Alle, die auf Klischees verzichten können
	www.ace-cafe-london.com		www.ace-cafe-london.com

Ace Cafe Reunion

The motorcycle is deemed to be a rebellious, anti-establishment statement. It's also young vs. old. Back in the 1960s, the mass-produced motorcycle that was individually remodeled into a race machine was something of a counterpart to today's cell phone. At that time, the social network didn't go by the name of Facebook; it was a street or a café. The kids met up with their bikes on the street or in cafés, just like the legendary Ace Cafe in Stonebridge, Northwest London, where biker small talk met with rock 'n' roll and coffee house culture, and *ta-dah*: A new concept of the café racer was born that has electrified motorcycling culture ever since. With the re-opening of the Ace Cafe in 2001, this culture is thriving again on the streets, and Stonebridge has been the epicenter for all those who have customizing ideas in their minds. A movement like this needs its own sacred festival: The Ace Cafe Reunion has existed since 1994; it's one of the biggest motorcycling rallies worldwide. It's about motorcycling, riders, speed, real content, geographical locations, and enjoying partying, riding, meeting up, watching people, and being watched. All the styles and models are welcome at the start of the Ace Cafe Reunion—be it café racers, classics, streetfighters, hypersport, bobbers, scramblers, roadsters, choppers, or cruisers. "Run what ya' brung!"—what really counts is the spirit, no matter what's roaring beneath ya'! If you feel like riding to the event, be sure to make a detour via the Café Hubraum in Solingen, Germany, the start of the Continental Run to London.

Das Motorrad als Ausdruck der Rebellion gegen das Establishment. Jung gegen Alt. Was heute das Handy, war in den Sechzigern das eigenhändig zur Rennmaschine umgebaute Serienmotorrad. Und weil das Social Network seinerzeit noch nicht Facebook hieß, sondern Straße und Café, trafen sich die Kids mit ihren Bikes auf der Straße und in Cafés wie eben dem legendären Ace Cafe in Stonebridge in Nordwest-London, wo Motorengeblubber auf Rock 'n' Roll und Kaffeehauskultur traf und jenen Begriff hervorbrachte, der seither die Anhänger der zweirädrigen Fahrkultur elektrisiert: Café Racer. Und weil eben diese Kultur wieder auf den Straßen der Erde aufblüht und seit der Wiedereröffnung des Ace Cafe in 2001 sein Epizentrum in Stonebridge hat, liegt hier das Mekka derjenigen, die den Begriff „Customizing" in ihrem Geist implantiert haben. Und weil solch eine Bewegung auch ihr heiliges Fest braucht, gibt's bereits seit 1994 die Ace Cafe Reunion, eines der größten Motorradtreffen weltweit überhaupt, bei dem es ums Motorradfahren, um Motorradfahrer, Speed, authentische Inhalte und Locations und den Spaß am Feiern, Abfahren, Treffen und Sehen-und-Gesehenwerden geht. Egal ob Café Racer, Classics, Streetfighter, HyperSport, Bobber, Scrambler, Roadster, Chopper oder Cruiser, bei der Ace Cafe Reunion sind alle Styles und alle Typen am Start. Was auch immer unter dem Hintern bollert – was zählt, ist der Spirit. Wer hinfahren will, macht am besten einen Umweg über Solingen, denn dort, im Café Hubraum, startet der Continental Run nach London.

"I'm not sure what cc is. But I can tell you, it's a proper bike and it's powerful."

Angelina Jolie (affirmation of an interviewer's question about Brad Pitt's birthday gift to her of the MV Agusta F4 CC)

Ich bin nicht sicher, was cc ist. Aber ich kann Ihnen sagen, es ist ein richtiges Motorrad, und es ist mächtig.

Angelina Jolie, in einem Interview, als sie darauf angesprochen wird, dass Brad Pitt ihr eine MV Agusta F4 CC zum Geburtstag geschenkt hat.

NEVER HAS THE URGE FOR INDIVIDUAL SELF-EXPRESSION BEEN MORE POPULAR THAN IT IS TODAY. BIKERS ARE NO DIFFERENT WHEN THEY USE THEIR CUSTOM BIKES TO ESCAPE THE MAINSTREAM VORTEX. PUTTING THEIR PASSION TO WORK, THESE GUYS HAVE BEEN KNOWN TO PRODUCE SOME TRULY REMARKABLE WORKS OF ART, FOR A PERFECT LIFESTYLE INVOLVES A LOT MORE THAN JUST TWO WHEELS. NOR IS THERE ANY SHORTAGE OF COOL SHOPS SPECIALIZING IN "A LOT MORE." THEIR DOORS ARE ALWAYS OPEN AS A SCENE HANGOUT, EVEN IF IT'S ONLY FOR THE OCCASIONAL CUP OF JOE. OR AS A PLACE FOR KINDRED SPIRITS TO COME HOME TO.

NIE STAND DAS BEDÜRFNIS NACH INDIVIDUELLER SELBSTENTFALTUNG SO HOCH IM KURS WIE HEUTE. AUCH BEI MOTORRADFAHRERN, DIE MIT IHREN CUSTOM BIKES GANZ EIGENE WEGE GEHEN, UM DEM SOG DES MAINSTREAMS ZU ENTRINNEN. WENN LEIDENSCHAFT PRODUKTIV WIRD, ENTSTEHEN BISWEILEN EINZIGARTIGE KUNSTWERKE. CHARAKTER MÜSSEN SIE HABEN. ABER ZUM PERFEKTEN LIFESTYLE GEHÖREN MEHR ALS NUR ZWEI RÄDER. FÜR DIESES „MEHR" GIBT ES COOLE SHOPS. GERNE AUCH ALS SZENETREFFS ODER FÜR DEN KAFFEE ZWISCHENDURCH. ODER EINFACH NUR ZUM HEIMKOMMEN.

Make My Day—Make My Bike

5

CUSTOM BIKES AND SHOPS

SAN BERNARDINO
Big Bear Choppers

Big Bear Choppers Motorcycles
1331 Riverview Drive
San Bernardino, CA 92408
USA
www.bigbearchoppers.com

The first time he was blown away wasn't when he met his wife, Mona; it was even before that when he discovered engines. Kevin Alsop, the boy from Melbourne, was just 15 when he handled, dismantled, and rebuilt his first one. Of course, it took some learning by working with his father, who was a professional racing rider. Years later, after the family had relocated from Australia to the US, he met Mona when he began to work in a small chopper store in L.A. That was the second time he was blown away. They got married and moved to the San Bernadino Mountains near Big Bear Lake which lent the company they founded in 1998 its name. Today, they build creative, well-crafted motorcycles for individualists. With about one hundred employees, they now offer more than ten model families. Their philosophy: One product made by one big family. That's the way to go for genuine quality.

Es war um ihn geschehen, sofort. Nicht nur bei seiner Frau Mona, sondern schon früher, bei den Motoren. Mit 15 bekam Kevin Alsop, der Junge aus Melbourne, zum ersten Mal einen in die Hände, baute ihn auseinander und wieder zusammen. Natürlich erst, nachdem er ihn zusammen mit seinem Vater, damals ein Profirennfahrer, noch ein bisschen verbessert hatte. Viele Jahre später, nachdem die Familie von Australien in die Vereinigten Staaten umgesiedelt war, lernte er Mona kennen, als er in L.A. in einem kleinen Chopper-Laden zu arbeiten anfing. Das zweite Mal war er hin und weg. Sie heirateten und zogen in die San-Bernadino-Berge in die Nähe des Big Bear Lake. Nach diesem benannten sie dann ihre 1998 gegründete Firma. Heute entwickeln sie kreative, gut gebaute Motorräder für Individualisten. Mit zirka hundert Mitarbeitern bieten sie mehr als zehn Modellfamilien an. Ihre Philosophie: ein Produkt, hergestellt von einer großen Familie. So muss es sein, und so bekommt man noch echte Qualität.

VENICE
Deus Ex Machina

Deus Ex Machina
1001 Venice Boulevard
Venice, CA 90291
USA
www.deuscustoms.com

Deus Ex Machina is a famous flagship address for custom bikes. There's a store on almost every continent—Sydney or Milan, Bali, or Byron Bay. And in Venice, L.A. This location is also one of the most vibrant hubs for surfing, biking, and motorcycling culture. Michael "Woolie" Woolway is king of the custom bikes here. He crafts them to perfection, also for celebrities like Ryan Reynolds and Billy Joel. The store is not only a workshop, the café is also a hip meeting point for surfers, bikers, and designers. Some only arrive for a coffee, others buy clothes, while others collect their handmade surfboard. Or one of Woolie's custom bikes.

Deus Ex Machina ist eine anerkannt feine Adresse für Custom Bikes. Ein Store findet sich auf fast jedem Kontinent. Sydney oder Mailand, Bali oder Byron Bay. Oder L.A., genauer: Venice. Dort ist einer der vibrierendsten Hubs des Surfens, Fahrradfahrens und der Motorradkultur. Michael „Woolie" Woolway ist dort der Herr über die Custom Bikes. Er feilt an ihnen, bis sie perfekt sind, auch für Prominente wie Ryan Reynolds und Billy Joel. Der Store ist aber nicht nur Werkstatt, das Café im Store ist auch ein Szenetreff für Surfer, Biker und Kreative. Manche kommen nur auf eine Tasse Kaffee hierher, andere kaufen sich Klamotten, wieder andere holen ihr handgemachtes Surfboard ab. Oder eben ein Custom Bike von Woolie.

ONLINESHOP
El Solitario

elsolitariomc.com

Biking is the pinnacle of speed. At least that's according to David Borras, owner of El Solitario. His home is the workshop. Here, somewhere in Galicia, he creates motorcycles that you either love or hate. There are no gray areas for him—it's just black and white. His bikes must have character; you have to feel alive on them and feel their fire in your belly. To make the biker lifestyle complete, Borras offers not just motorcycles, but also clothing, accessories, and everything that makes bikers' hearts skip a beat. It's important for him to offer handmade products only from Spain or Portugal that are produced in traditional family companies. To him, the fine details are just as important as the overall picture. Which is exactly the way he handles all his bikes. After all, "motorcycles are the last bastion of freedom."

Motorradfahren ist der Inbegriff von Geschwindigkeit. Sagt zumindest David Borras, Herr über El Solitario. Sein Zuhause: die Werkstatt. Dort, irgendwo in Galizien, kreiert er Motorräder, die man entweder liebt oder hasst. Bei ihm gibt es kein Grau, nur Schwarz und Weiß. Charakter müssen seine Bikes haben, man soll sich auf ihnen lebendig fühlen und ihr Feuer im Bauch spüren. Um den richtigen Biker-Lifestyle komplett zu machen, bietet Borras nicht nur Motorräder an, sondern auch Klamotten, Accessoires und alles andere, was das Bikerherz höher schlagen lässt. Ihm ist wichtig, nur Handmade-Artikel aus Spanien oder Portugal anzubieten, die in traditionellen Familienunternehmen gefertigt werden. Es sind die Details, die ihm wichtig sind. So wie bei seinen Bikes. Denn: „Motorräder sind die letzte Bastion der Freiheit."

Iron & Resin

Iron & Resin San Fransisco
7 Columbus Avenue
San Francisco, CA 94111
USA
www.ironandresin.com

A shopping area of 14,000 square feet. Not too big, not too small, just right. The store has all the apparel to make bikers' hearts skip a beat. Iron & Resin offers almost everything from clothes to accessories and kitchenware: bikers' kitchenware. Iron & Resin's second shop is located in the historic building of the Bank of Italy in San Francisco's trendy North Beach neighborhood. If you prefer surfing to biking, you'll also find what you're looking for. Three friends from southern California founded the company. Three friends, who believe in selling products not made by the disposable world of mass production.

Shoppen auf 1300 m². Nicht zu groß, nicht zu klein. Gerade richtig, um das anzubieten, was das Bikerherz höher schlagen lässt. Bei Iron & Resin gibt es nahezu alles, von Klamotten über Accessoires bin hin zu Küchensachen. Also Biker-Küchensachen. Untergebracht ist der zweite Shop von Iron & Resin im historischen Gebäude der Bank of Italy in San Franciscos Szeneviertel North Beach. Auch wer kein Biker ist, sondern lieber aufs Surfbrett springt, findet was. Gegründet wurde das Unternehmen von drei Freunden aus dem Süden von Kalifornien. Den dreien ist es wichtig, keine Wegwerfprodukte aus der Massenfabrikation zu verkaufen.

COPENHAGEN
Jamesville Motorcycles

46 Matthæusgade
1666 Copenhagen
Denmark
customsfromjamesville.blogspot.dk

Denmark isn't his home country, but it is his new home. James Roper-Caldbeck is from England, but he has settled in Copenhagen—and naturally, a girl enticed him here. So it was too late when he realized that Denmark is arguably the worst country to offer custom bikes in. But he's succeeded, anyway. Today he has a small shop restoring vintage Harley-Davidsons from the 1930s through the 1980s. His customers trust him implicitly, and not just in Denmark. They deliver their bikes to James and only see them again once the build job is finished. Upon collection, so far, everyone has climbed on his or her bike with a beaming face. James rebuilds the bikes to reveal their true magic.

Dänemark ist zwar nicht sein Heimatland, aber sein neues Zuhause. James Roper-Caldbeck kommt aus England, hat sich aber in Kopenhagen niedergelassen. Dorthin gelockt hat ihn natürlich ein Mädchen. Zu spät stellte er fest, dass Dänemark das denkbar schlechteste Land war, um Custom Bikes anzubieten. Er hat es trotzdem geschafft. Heute betreibt er dort einen kleinen Laden, in dem er alte Harley-Davidsons aus den Dreißiger- bis Achtzigerjahren restauriert. Interessenten für seine Arbeit findet er nicht nur in Dänemark. Seine Kunden vertrauen ihm blind, sie geben ihr Motorrad bei James ab und bekommen es erst wieder zu Gesicht, wenn er damit fertig ist. Alle sind bisher beim Abholen mit einem strahlenden Gesicht auf ihr Bike gestiegen. Denn James lockt aus den Maschinen etwas ganz Besonderes heraus.

BROOKLYN
Union Garage

103 Union Street
Brooklyn, New York City 11231
USA
uniongaragenyc.com

They're in good company in this neighborhood: Next door to Moto Borgotaro, the European vintage bikes repair and restoration shop, furthermore sharing the same block with Moto Pistole, the area's modern Ducati service shop. Union Garage sales rooms are located right in the center. This is Brooklyn's coolest address for bikers. It's not just a shop, it's also a meeting point, and a party place. Incidentally, the shop is not only open during usual business hours, but also by appointment. The store offers all the hippest and the best of bike accessories and apparel. They even provide touring tips. What makes this shop so practical is that the inside of the bricks-and-mortar is staunchly vintage, while its online shop has come into its own in the bright new world of Internet shopping.

In solch einer Nachbarschaft lässt es sich gut hausen. Nebenan schrauben die Jungs von Moto Borgotaro an europäischen Vintage Bikes herum, im selben Block residiert mit Moto Pistole der modernste Ducati-Shop weit und breit, und mittendrin hat die Union Garage ihre Verkaufsräume. Das ist Brooklyns coolste Adresse für Biker, nicht nur Shop, sondern auch Treffpunkt und Partylocation. Der Shop schließt übrigens nicht nur zu den üblichen Ladenöffnungszeiten seine Türen auf, sondern auch nach Terminvereinbarung. Alles, was in Sachen Bike-Accessoires Rang und Namen hat, steht hier im Regal. Tourentipps gibt's hier auch. Und das Praktische an diesem Laden: Innendrin ist er zwar verdammt vintage, nach außen mit seinem Online-Shop aber voll und ganz in der schönen neuen Welt des Internets angekommen.

Industrial designer Chad Hodge had the painful experience that old love sometimes rusts. When Chad bought his first motorcycle, a Kawasaki KZ 750 B, ten years ago, it was in a condition that only vaguely resembled the original 1978 model. So it was time for action. Chad rebuilt the engine, then started on the frame: "Full rebuild" was his motto. His mission was to remake the rear of the bike from the ground up, making space for the battery and rear lights. The rider is also treated to plenty of space on a luxurious, beige leather seat that makes a stylish contrast to the gray tone of the tank.

Alte Liebe rostet eben doch, wie der Industriedesigner Chad Hodge eines Tages schmerzlich feststellen musste. Seine Kawasaki KZ 750 B, sein erstes Motorrad, hatte er rund zehn Jahre zuvor gekauft. In einem Zustand, der nur noch vage an den des Ursprungmodells von 1978 erinnerte. Es war Zeit zu handeln. Chad erneuerte den Motor und legte Hand an den Rahmen: Alles neu – so die Devise. Es galt, das Heck von Grund auf zu modellieren, damit Batterie und Rücklichter Platz fanden. Platz findet aber auch der Fahrer: Und zwar auf einer edlen Lederbank, die farblich Akzente setzt und sich so stilvoll vom ergrauten Tank abhebt.

KAWASAKI KZ 750 B CUSTOMIZED
Chad Hodge

www.chadhodgedesign.com

DP Customs

www.dpcustomcycles.com

Long ago in Denver, they raced an exhilarating circuit. One day a rider asked, "would you guys be game to build a bike that's insanely fast?" That was clearly a rhetorical question. Jarrod and Justin Del Prado, the brothers at the helm of DP Customs, feel best when they're pushing the boundaries of speed, so they passionately accepted the challenge. They created the Turbo Destroyer, a 154-hp drag bike, which was built to clear specifications: ultra long, ultra lightweight, and ultra fast. The centerpiece of the hell-raising machine is a turbo-charged 1,200-cc engine made by Trask Performance, while the fork is from a Ducati 1198 S and the tires are from Pirelli.

Es war eine muntere Runde, damals, irgendwann in Denver. Bis ein Rennfahrer fragte: „Would you guys be game to build a bike that's insanely fast?" Eine rhetorische Frage, klar. Und weil die Del-Prado-Brüder Jarrod und Justin von DP Customs sich am Rande des Geschwindigkeitswahnsinns bestens aufgehoben fühlen, nahmen sie die Herausforderung mit Handkuss an. So entstand der Turbo Destroyer, ein 154 PS starkes Drag Bike, das nach klar formulierten Anforderungen konstruiert wurde: extrem lang, extrem leicht, extrem schnell. Das Herzstück der Höllenmaschine bildet ein turbogeladener 1200-cm³-Motor von Trask Performance, die Motorradgabel stammt von einer Ducati 1198 S, das Paar Reifen von Pirelli.

Ed Turner Motorcycles

www.edturner-motorcycles.com

The Silver Raven is based on a BMW R 65 model from 1979. Apart from the brand emblem on the tank and boxer engine, not much remains of the original bike. Karl Renoult, the design genius behind Ed Turner Motorcycles, handled the rebuild exceptionally. The client had a clear vision: radical and unique—that was his aim for the bike. The double disc brakes are from a Kawasaki Z 1000. The same goes for the upside-down fork and brake calipers. The other Silver Raven parts like the wheels or wings were taken from a police-reformed R 1150 motorcycle. The final piece is from a Honda CB 400.

Der Silver Raven basiert auf einer BMW R 65 von 1979. Doch bis auf das am Tank angebrachte Markenemblem und den Boxermotor ist vom Ursprungsmodell nur wenig übrig geblieben. Damit erfüllte Karl Renoult, der Kopf hinter Ed Turner Motorcycles, seinen Job mit Bravour. Der Kunde hatte nämlich klare Vorstellungen: Radikal und einzigartig – so sollte das Bike aussehen. Die Doppelscheibenbremsen stammen daher von einer Kawasaki Z 1000, ebenso die Upside-down-Gabel und die Bremszangen. Weitere Teile, wie Räder oder Schwinge, erhielt der Silver Raven von einer ausgeschlachteten R 1150, die einst im Dienst der Polizei stand. Das Endstück wiederum kommt von einer Honda CB 400.

Long, flat, monochrome, and aggressive: Probably the best intercontinental styles are established in a Dresden workshop with a clear vision of how to finish a Honda CB 750. The Hookie Co. workshop started this project by breaking down the Honda to release the machine's true potential. The polished frame was then treated to a coat of high-gloss black paint, while a new LED strip was added as rear lighting. The team's rebuild strategy made the best visual use of the Honda's original parts. The remodeled tank is striking with its minimalist design and urban look. The perfect finishing touch is the refashioned seat with its supercool combination of leather and denim.

Lang, flach, monochrom und aggressiv: Wenn man sich in Dresden mit klaren Vorstellungen eine Honda CB 750 zur Brust nimmt, ist das die wohl schönste Art der interkontinentalen Beziehungspflege. So machte sich das Team um Hookie Co. also an die Arbeit, zerlegte die Honda erst in ihre Einzelteile und befreite sie dann von unnötigem Ballast. Der geschliffene Rahmen erhielt eine schwarze Hochglanzlackierung, das Rücklicht wurde mit LED-Streifen aufgehübscht. Überhaupt brachten die Jungs durch ihre Veredlungsmaßnahmen so ziemlich alles optisch auf Trab, was die Honda an Teilen hergab. Ein besonderer Eyecatcher: der Tank, der durch minimalistisches Design und seine urbane Symbolik ins Auge springt. Da passt es natürlich vorzüglich, dass die umgemodelte Sitzbank in einem coolen Denim-Leder-Mix daherkommt.

HONDA CB 750 K(Z): HOOKIE VI

Hookie Co.

www.hookie.co

Steve McQueen personifies the style of the 1960s like no one else. Dirk Oehlerking pays tribute to the Hollywood star—and takes a trip down memory lane—with a reinterpretation of the Triumph Scrambler 900. Powered by an air-cooled 865-cc engine, the newly named "Il Sardo" races straight toward its cult bike status. This good-looking, off-road Triumph weighs in at a lighter 416 pounds and has upgraded Mitas tires with telescopic front fork that Oehlerking fitted with stiffer shocks. The rebuilt, hand-polished frame with nickel plating also has star quality.

Wie kein Zweiter verkörpert Steve McQueen den Stil der Sechziger. Dirk Oehlerking zollt der Filmikone daher Tribut – und weckt die wilde Zeit mit einer Neuinterpretation der Triumph Scrambler 900 aus ihrem Schönheitsschlaf. Angefeuert von einem luftgekühlten 865-cm³-Zweizylindermotor prescht die sogenannte „Il Sardo" zielsicher in Richtung Kultstatus. Dabei ist ihr eigentlich das Gelände lieber. Dort macht die 189 Kilo schwere Triumph mit ihren Mitas-Reifen und einer Telegabel, die Oehlerking mit härteren Federn ausgestattet hat, eine besonders gute Figur. Auch wegen des modifizierten Rahmens, der einen Nickelüberzug erhielt und derart veredelt für ein optisches Highlight sorgt.

TRIUMPH SCRAMBLER 900: IL SARDO
Kingston Custom

www.kingstoncustom.blogspot.com

A client rebuilt the parts of his BMW R 75/6, but he wanted a custom seat. For that, he contacted the Maria Riding Company. It quickly became clear to them that this project was much more ambitious than making a new seat! After one look at the worn-out BMW, the Portuguese custom bike experts began a major rethink, and developed a design that the amateur mechanic couldn't refuse. The innovative, custom-built remodel was less ambitious, yet had more attitude. Its Firestone tires were paired with sporty aluminum rims, while the frame gave the new bike a fearless look. Some components were concealed behind a panel combining classic and feisty elements. Today this custom bike cruises the streets by the name of "Panzer" (tank).

Der Kunde hatte hier und da schon ein wenig an seiner BMW R 75/6 herumgeschraubt. Was allerdings noch fehlte, war die passende Sitzbank. Um die Lücke zu schließen, wandte er sich an die Maria Riding Company. Schnell wurde klar: Bei einer Sitzbank würde es nicht bleiben. Der portugiesische Experte für Motorradumbauten nahm sich der abgelebten BMW mit dem Blick fürs große Ganze an und entwarf ein Konzept, das der Hobbyschrauber nicht ablehnen konnte. So entstand eine ausgefallene Neuinterpretation, kleiner, aber zugleich aggressiver im Auftritt. Die Firestone-Reifen erhielten sportliche Leichtmetallfelgen, während sich durch den komplett erneuerten Rahmen ein robuster Look zieht. Verschiedene Teile verschwanden hinter einer Verkleidung, die klassische mit aggressiven Elementen vereint. Heute rollt das modifizierte Bike deshalb auch unter dem Namen „Panzer" über die Straßen.

BMW R 75/6: PANZER
Maria Riding Company

www.maria-ridingcompany.com

Orange County Choppers

www.orangecountychoppers.com

With upper arms like tree trunks and covered in tattoos, plus his goatee beard, he looks something like a walrus: Paul Teutul, Sr. trades on his unmistakable tough guy image that seems designed to reflect the quality workmanship of his custom motorcycles. 65-year-old Paul and his son, Paul Teutul, Jr., are joint owners of Orange County Choppers. Their success was so phenomenal that almost five years ago, Mercedes AMG arrived on their doorstep to order an AMG Chopper. To boost sales for what was the then new SLS Class, OCC created a chopper with an independently suspended tank that is based on the original motor hood design. The three-part chrome wheels held together with sixty screws are a clear reference to AMG. The 24-inch front wheel is just as impressive as the lightweight OCC frame under which lurks an upgraded 1,647-cc S&S engine.

Oberarme im Baumstammformat, dazu Tattoos und ein Bart, der stark an ein Walross erinnert: Paul Teutul Senior pflegt einen kernigen Look, unverwechselbar und geradezu so, also reflektiere er damit den Charakter seiner Custom Bikes. Gemeinsam mit seinem Sohn Paul Teutul Junior betreibt der 65-Jährige erfolgreich die Motorradschmiede Orange County Choppers. So erfolgreich, dass vor rund fünf Jahren der Mercedes-Veredler AMG vor der Tür stand und einen AMG-Chooper in Auftrag gab. Zur Bewerbung des damals neuen SLS entstand so ein Chopper, dessen freischwebender Tank im Motorhaubendesign daherkommt. Die dreiteiligen, mit sechzig Schrauben verbundenen Chromräder nehmen unverkennbar Bezug auf AMG. Dabei wirkt das 24-Zoll-Vorderrad ebenso imposant wie der filigrane OCC-Rahmen, unter dem ein S&S-Motor mit 1647 cm³ auf seinen Einsatz lauert.

Just as James Bond orders his Martinis shaken, but not stirred, Shaw Speed & Custom specifies procedures that lend cutting edge refinements to its custom-built bike series. The Martini Bikes were launched in 2013 to celebrate the 150th anniversary of the Martini brand. The limited edition sportsters in striking "pearl white" and "flat silver" colors have a lean RSD tank. The British motorcycling experts have also rebuilt the exhaust system, brakes, and front wheel suspension. The bikes are based on a Harley XL 883 R and feature a classic Martini racing outfit, while the power has been increased with a Screamin' Eagle engine.

So wie James Bond sein Lieblingsgetränk durch gleichmäßiges Schütteln verfeinert, so hat auch Shaw Speed & Custom ein Veredlungsverfahren entwickelt, um Bandproduktionen den letzten Schliff zu verleihen. Die Martini Bikes entstanden im Jahr 2013 anlässlich des 150. Jubiläums der gleichnamigen Spirituosenmarke. Die Sportster, streng limitiert und in den Farbvarianten „Pearl White" und „Flat Silver" erhältlich, setzen auf einen schlanken RSD-Tank, wobei der britische Motorradexperte ebenso Auspuffanlage, Bremsen und Vorderradaufhängung in Angriff nahm. Beide Bikes basieren auf einer Harley XL 883 R, kommen im klassischen Martini-Racing-Outfit daher und werden von einem Screamin'-Eagle-Motor angetrieben.

HARLEY-DAVIDSON XL 883 R
MARTINI MOTORCYCLE
Shaw Speed & Custom

www.shawspeedandcustom.co.uk

Stefano Venier was always happiest when he stayed away from asphalt routes. So it was a perfect match when the Italian Carabinieri handed him a Moto Guzzi 750 cc. Venier, a native-born Italian based in New York, rebuilt the original model in several stages to create a Moto Guzzi Scrambler—the culmination of a childhood dream. Stefano always enjoys off-roading, whether earlier on his moped or today on the Tractor V 75. His customized Scrambler comes with a handmade, military style aluminum tank and features an ammunition case on the side of the leather seat and double front lights. Rustic shocks and wide Vee Rubber tires round off this stylish machine.

Stefano Venier fand sein Glück schon immer abseits geteerter Wege. Und so kam es mehr als gelegen, als ihm aus Polizeibesitz eine Moto Guzzi 750 cc in die Hände fiel. Venier, Italiener mit Sitz in New York, baute das Ursprungsmodell in mehreren Schritten zum Scrambler um. Ein Kindheitstraum, den er sich selbst erfüllte. Stefano machte schon immer gerne das Gelände unsicher. Damals auf dem Moped, heute auf dem Tractor V 75: Der Scrambler Marke Eigenbau kommt mit handgefertigtem Aluminiumtank im Military-style, daher trägt seitlich am Ledersitz einen Munitionskasten und vorn zwei große Scheinwerfer. Eine rustikale Federung sowie breite Vee-Rubber-Reifen runden das Erscheinungsbild stilvoll ab.

MOTO GUZZI NTX 750 CC: TRACTOR V75
Venier Customs

www.venier-customs.com

Wrenchmonkees

www.wrenchmonkees.com

Leslie from Estonia loved the sound of his Laverda, which always suggested a sweet getaway on boundless joy rides. All he needed was the right look, so he gave the Wrenchmonkees the restyling job. The Danish experts skillfully removed as many of the excess components as possible to expose the original aesthetics of the two-cylinder engine. Modern elements like speedometer, turn signals, and exhaust were brought out, while the aluminum tank caused a sensation. In contrast to the brash, industrial look are the quilted leather seat and finely orchestrated aluminum handlebar. The custom refit was a success — the mythical Laverda was reborn!

Für Leslie aus Estland klang der Sound seiner Laverda schon immer wie die süße Verheißung eines grenzenlosen Fahrvergnügens. Fehlte eben nur noch die passende Optik. Und die gab er bei Wrenchmonkees in Auftrag. Mit geschultem Händchen entfernten die Dänen so viel Überflüssiges wie möglich, um die Schönheit des Zweizylindermotors freizulegen. Moderne Züge manifestieren sich in Tacho, Blinker und Auspuff, wobei besonders der Aluminiumtank für Aussehen sorgt. Die gesteppte Ledersitzbank und der fein inszenierte Alulenker setzen der ruppigen Anmut des Industrielooks einen stimmigen Kontrast entgegen. Ein rundum gelungener Umbau, der den Mythos Laverda zu neuem Leben erweckt.

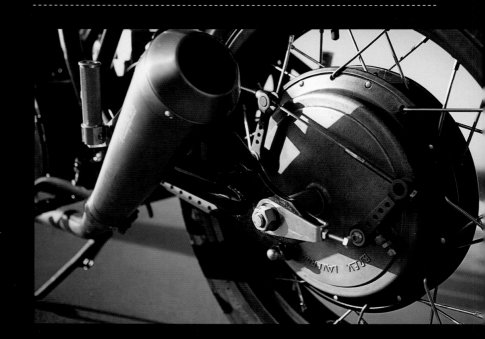

IMPRINT

© 2015 teNeues Media GmbH + Co. KG, Kempen

EDITORIAL STAFF: Eckhard Grauer, Bernd Haase, Matthias Mederer, Alexander Morath, Christina Rahmes, Winni Scheibe
DESIGN CONCEPT & ART DIRECTION:
MAGNETIC STORIES (Lutz Suendermann & Oliver Semik)
LAYOUT: STAN STUDIOS www.stan-studios.com
PHOTO EDITOR: Antonietta Procopio
INTRODUCTION: Michael Köckritz,
Red Indians Publishing GmbH & Co. KG
EDITORIAL MANAGEMENT TENEUES:
Regine Freyberg & Arndt Jasper, teNeues Media GmbH + Co. KG
TRANSLATIONS: Artes Translations, Dr Suzanne Kirkbright,
American English translations by Conan Kirkpatrick
PROOFREADING: Mareike Ahlborn
PREPRESS: STAN STUDIOS
PRODUCTION: Alwine Krebber, teNeues Media GmbH + Co. KG

PUBLISHED BY TENEUES PUBLISHING GROUP

teNeues Media GmbH + Co. KG
Am Selder 37, 47906 Kempen, Germany
Phone: +49 (0)2152 916 0
Fax: +49 (0)2152 916 111
e-mail: books@teneues.com

Press department: Andrea Rehn
Phone: +49 (0)2152 916 202
e-mail: arehn@teneues.com

teNeues Publishing Company
7 West 18th Street, New York, NY 10011, USA
Phone: +1 212 627 9090
Fax: +1 212 627 9511

teNeues Publishing UK Ltd.
12 Ferndene Road, London SE24 0AQ, UK
Phone: +44 (0)20 3542 8997

teNeues France S.A.R.L.
39, rue des Billets, 18250 Henrichemont, France
Phone: +33 (0)2 48 26 93 48
Fax: +33 (0)1 70 72 34 82

www.teneues.com

ISBN: 978-3-8327-3250-9
Library of Congress Control Number: 2014958819
Printed in the Czech Republic

CREDITS

COVER   Scott G. Toepfer

PAGE 004–005:
Laurent Nivalle
PAGE 006–007: Laurent Nivalle
PAGE 008–009:
Bob Thomas Sports Photography
PAGE 012: Laurent Nivalle
PAGE 014–015: Laurent Nivalle
PAGE 016–017: Laurent Nivalle
PAGE 026–027: Getty Images
PAGE 038–039: Getty Images /
www.motorcycle.com
PAGE 052–053: Getty Images
PAGE 070–071: Getty Images
PAGE 088–089: Getty Images
PAGE 102–103: Getty Images
PAGE 118–119: Getty Images
PAGE 124–125: Getty Images
PAGE 126–127: Laurent Nivalle
PAGE 128–129: Scott G. Toepfer
PAGE 133: Laurent Nivalle
PAGE 135: Manuel Marabese /
Edelweiß Bike Travel Reise gesGmbH
PAGE 136: Alan Magnoni /
Edelweiß Bike Travel Reise gesGmbH
PAGE 140: Werner Wachter /
Edelweiß Bike Travel Reise gesGmbH
PAGE 142–143: Werner Wachter /
Edelweiß Bike Travel Reise gesGmbH
PAGE 144–145: Laurent Nivalle
PAGE 148–149: Laurent Nivalle
PAGE 150–151: Laurent Nivalle
PAGE 152–153:
The Distinguished Gentleman's Ride
PAGE 154–155: Bundesverband der
Motorradfahrer e.V. (BVDM)
PAGE 156–157: Laurent Nivalle
PAGE 158–159: Laurent Nivalle
PAGE 160–163: Armin Adams
PAGE 164–165: Motorcycle Film Festival
PAGE 166–167: Deus Ex Machina
PAGE 168–171: Martin Kuschel / Photostars
Berlin / Ace Cafe London GmbH
PAGE 172–177: Scott Toepfer
PAGE 181: Union Garage

PAGE 182–183: Big Bear Choppers
PAGE 184–185: Scott G. Toepfer
PAGE 186–187: Kristina Fender
PAGE 188–189: Samson Hatae
PAGE 190–191: Jamesville Motorcycles
PAGE 192–193: Union Garage / Blaine Davis
PAGE 194–195: David Ohl
PAGE 197–199: Blaine Davis
PAGE 200–201: DP Custom Cycles
PAGE 202–205: Pierre Le Targat
PAGE 206: Felix Meyer
PAGE 207: Thomas Schlorke
PAGE 208–209: David Ohl
PAGE 210–211: Kingston Custom
PAGE 212–213: Maria Riding Company
PAGE 214–215: factstudio
(www.factstudio.de)
PAGE 216–217: Shaw Speed & Custom
PAGE 218–219: Donatello Trevisiol
PAGE 220–221: Wrenchmonkees
PAGE 222–223: David Ohl

Aprilia, Benelli, Bimota, BMW Group,
BMW Motorrad, BSA, Ducati, Harley-Davidson,
Honda, Indian, Kawasaki, Laverda,
Moto Guzzi, Moto Morini, Münch, MV Agusta,
Norton, Suzuki, Scott G. Toepfer, Triumph,
Yamaha

Armin Adams, Blaine Davis, David Ohl,
Donatello Trevisiol, DP Custom Cycles,
factstudio (www.factstudio.de), Kingston
Custom, Maria Riding Company, Martin
Kuschel / Photostars Berlin und Ace Cafe
London GmbH, Pierre Le Targat, Shaw Speed &
Custom, Terry Richardson, The Distinguished
Gentleman's Ride, Thomas Schlorke,
Wrenchmonkees

With the kind support of Laurent Nivalle,
Scott G. Toepfer, Winni Scheibe (www.winni-
scheibe.de) and the Motor Presse Stuttgart
GmbH + Co. KG / Red. Motorrad. Thanks for
your great pictures!